Martingale
& COMPANY

Bothell, Washington

Fantasy Fabrics

Bonnie Lyn McCaffery

FIBER STUDIO PRESS

Fiber Studio Press is an imprint of
Martingale & Company.

Credits

President .... Nancy J. Martin
CEO/Publisher .... Daniel J. Martin
Associate Publisher .... Jane Hamada
Editorial Director .... Mary V. Green
Technical Editor .... Ursula Reikes
Cover and Text Designer .... Cheryl Stevenson
Copy Editor .... Liz McGehee
Illustrator .... Mario Ferro
Photographer .... Brent Kane

Fantasy Fabrics
© 1999 by Bonnie Lyn McCaffery
Martingale & Company, PO Box 118,
Bothell, WA 98041-0118 USA

Printed in Hong Kong
04 03 02 01 00 99   6 5 4 3 2 1

Library of Congress Cataloging-in-Publication Data
McCaffery, Bonnie Lyn,
   Fantasy fabrics / Bonnie Lyn McCaffery.
      p.   cm.
   Includes bibliographical references.
   ISBN 1-56477-272-1
   1. Quilting. 2. Quilts—Design. 3. Textile fabrics in art.
I. Title.
TT834.M2739   1999
746.46—DC21   99-34070
                                                           CIP

Mission Statement

We are dedicated to providing quality products and service by working together to inspire creativity and to enrich the lives we touch.

Dedication

I have three wonderful daughters: Heather, Carly, and Abby. Heather has always had an eye for color and is always willing to help when I'm not sure. Carly inspires me to continue learning. Abby encourages me to reach for my goals as she does in her cross-country track and skiing. This book is dedicated to them and, most of all, to my husband, Michael. He has given me the freedom to be an artist. Whenever I say I want to do something, he always urges me to go ahead and do it. He gave up his garage so I could have a place to call my own—a studio to develop ideas, classes, lectures, quilts, and now a book.

I would be nowhere without the help and support of these wonderful people. It is to them that I dedicate this book.

Acknowledgments

Thank you to all those generous people who loaned me their pieces: Barbara Anderson, Laurie D. Calvitti, Marie B. DiGerlando, Julie Duschack, Shelby M. Gallagher, Judy Zoelzer Levine, Helen P. Marinaro, Heather Lyn McCaffery, Linda M. Poole, Kathleen Oehlmann, Kathleen Porycki, Sharon Lee Williams, and Katherine Worthington. Sharon Lee Williams also inspired me to incorporate silk flowers, and Barbara Anderson suggested the use of doll hair.

Thank you to Nancy Morgan, Stephanie Savage, Linda Poole, and Sharla Hicks—my cheerleading section—who are always urging me forward and supporting me in moments of panic. Thank you to the members of the Milford Valley Quilters for their continued support, their willingness to act as my testing lab for workshops, and their terrific suggestions.

Thanks to my mom, Norma Giancone, who continuously proofed my work and smoothed it all out to be reader-friendly.

I would like to thank the following companies for their generous support: Creative Crystals; Hoffman Fabrics; Springs Fabrics; Z-Barten Productions; Freudenberg Non-Wovens; Wrights; Kreinik Manufacturing Co., Inc.; YLI Corporation; Sulky of America; JHB International Buttons; Omnigrid, Inc.; Fiskars, Inc.; Prym-Dritz Corporation; and Reliance Trading Corporation of America (silk flowers).

Thank you also to the staff at Martingale & Company, a wonderful group of people to work with.

Table of Contents

Preface

Like most quilters, I love fabric, not just cottons, but any kind of fabric—silks, metallics, organzas, satins, Ultra Suede. You name it, I probably love it and own some. I love color, design, luster, and texture. I love sheer fabrics and how they interact with each other as they are layered. This love of fabrics drew me into the process of creating fantasy fabrics.

Experimenting with the process satisfies my need for quick gratification. While I admire quilts that take months and years to create, it is not in my nature to spend so much of my time on one project. I love the complexity of quilts with numerous curved pieces, but I am not one that relishes the process of turning under all of those tiny edges. I wanted a way to speed up the process. So, combining this need for quick gratification and my love of sheers, fantasy fabrics was born.

Cutting, positioning, and capturing various items on a base fabric creates these beautiful fabrics. Held in place under a layer of tulle, these items are then stitched to the base fabric. When I started experimenting with cut shapes, I quickly realized there were many more things that could be captured under the top layer of tulle. While the technique is similar to shadow quilting, it has been revamped and brought into the next millennium, incorporating all kinds of fun things. No longer are we restrained by rules and limited fabric choices. What a great time to be into quilting!

Introduction

Fantasy fabrics—oh the possibilities!

The technique is playful, liberating, and the resulting wonderful new fabric can be used for piecing, appliqué, and backgrounds for other quilts, or framed as pieces of art. Imagine using feathers, glitter shapes, decorative threads, or cutup fabrics and capturing them underneath tulle.

This book includes step-by-step directions to create one simple piece of fantasy fabric. Once you understand the process, the sections that follow suggest numerous variations, from different fabrics and threads you can use to the many items you can capture between the layers. Any tips I've come across while creating these variations are included so you can learn from my experience. The final section discusses ways to use these wonderful fabrics, from pieced and appliquéd quilts to clothing and accessories. Read on and be inspired to create fantasy fabrics.

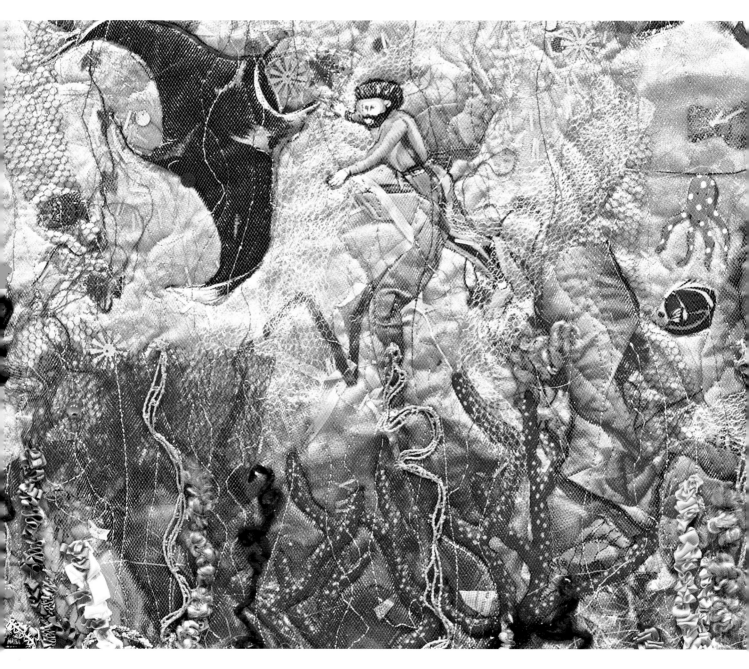

Fabrics

First of all, you need a base fabric on which to assemble the captured items and a sheer top fabric to hold the items in place. Cotton works well for the base. Tulle is a good choice for the top fabric. Alternatives for both the base fabric and top fabric will be discussed further in the "Experimenting with Fabrics" section.

Stabilizers

A firm tear-away stabilizer such as Pellon Stitch-n-Tear or Sulky Stiffy will keep the fabric flat while stitching the layers together. I like Pellon Stitch-n-Tear. It is available by the yard for larger pieces, and has a stiffness that helps me maneuver the piece while stitching. Smaller pieces of stabilizer can be basted together to form a larger piece.

Supplies

- Pins are needed to hold the layers together. I like bright, large-headed pins because they are easy to see and grasp while stitching.

- A sewing machine is the best way to stitch the layers together. A large, empty work space is necessary to support the layers while stitching. A walking foot and a darning foot are also helpful. Someone always asks me, "Can I do this by hand?" I will certainly not hold them back from trying, but I feel it is much easier and faster to stitch the layers together by machine. For those who prefer handwork, feel free to do it by hand.

- A rotary cutter with a sharp blade, rotary rulers, and a rotary-cutting mat are useful for cutting fabrics. A standard-size (28mm) rotary cutter will allow for tighter curves, and a small (11" x 17") rotary-cutting mat will be more convenient to turn. The rotary cutter is a very sharp tool and should be treated with great respect. Always cut in a comfortable position, turning the cutting mat as necessary to continue in a comfortable position. Keep your fingers out of the path of the rotary cutter. DO NOT cut toward yourself. And ALWAYS close the blade cover when not in use.

- An iron and ironing surface are needed to press fabrics flat. Always test unusual fabrics before pressing the finished fantasy fabric piece. Many of the unusual fabrics and items will melt under higher temperatures, so it is best to use a medium to low temperature setting. It is also a good idea to press the fantasy fabrics from the wrong side. If the piece contains some unusual items like feathers, sequins, metallic confetti, or plastic-coated ribbons, be sure to protect the ironing surface with a plain piece of copier paper.

- Heavy-duty spray starch is used to stabilize the fabric for stitching.

- A reducing lens, a camera, a peephole for a door, or binoculars is helpful for previewing the design. Any of these tools reduces the image and allows you to see the design from a distance. Look through the wrong end of the binoculars to see a reduced view. Peepholes for doors are available in hardware stores.

- Tweezers are helpful in removing tiny bits of stabilizer or tracing paper.

Captured Items

Many different items can be incorporated into fantasy fabric. Cut fabric shapes, threads, ribbons, metallic confetti shapes, lace, glitter, charms, and beads are just a few of the items that will be covered in detail later.

The Basic Steps

Let's start by doing one simple piece of fantasy fabric in order to understand the process. It is best to get comfortable stitching on a smaller piece before attempting to make a larger piece. A fat quarter or smaller is a good size to start with. Once you are comfortable maneuvering this size in the sewing machine, you can try larger pieces. I find 40" to be about the largest size I can handle in the sewing machine.

1. Start with a fat quarter (18" x 22") or a fat eighth (9" x 22" or 11" x 18") of cotton for the base fabric. Spray the back of the fabric with heavy-duty spray starch and press flat to keep the fabric firm and flat while stitching. Thoroughly inspect and remove any lint or dust from the base fabric.

2. Cut a piece of tear-away stabilizer slightly larger than the base fabric and press it with an iron so it will lie flat. Place the stabilizer under the base fabric.

3. Cut a piece of tulle the same size as the base fabric. Press the tulle, using a cool to medium temperature setting. (Test a small corner of the tulle for the correct temperature.) Set the tulle aside.

4. Now the fun begins. Work on a flat surface. Select some sheer fabrics for cut shapes. You can use tulle, organza, lace, and a variety of other sheer and transparent fabrics. Avoid fabrics that unravel easily unless you want this effect. Try out fabrics on the base fabric before cutting any shapes. Notice how the colors of the intended shapes interact with the color of the base fabric.

5. Play with it. Cut some shapes using a rotary cutter and mat. Some possible shapes are squares, triangles, teardrops, or moon slivers. Try to cut the curved shapes in one continuous motion if possible. Instead of picking up the blade when you want to cut in another direction, leave the blade in place and turn the mat before continuing to cut.

    You can use a rotary ruler along with the cutter to get a curved edge, but it isn't necessary. If you are inexperienced with the rotary cutter, use the ruler to keep the cutter from slipping into your fingers.

6. Cut several shapes in different sizes and colors. Arrange the shapes on the base fabric, individually or in groups, overlapping them if desired. Experiment with combining colors and creating transparencies. Cut more shapes as needed to fill out the design.

7. Preview your design to get a better idea of how it will look from a distance. Use a reducing tool (page 7) or stand back and squint. By viewing the design from a distance, any fabrics, shapes, or colors that need to be changed will stand out. It is much easier to change them now before all the layers are pinned together. When you are happy with the layout, carefully look over the surface for any undesirable threads, lint, or stray fuzz. Once trapped by the top layer, they will be a permanent part of the fabric, so remove them now. Place the reserved layer of tulle on top. Smooth everything into place.

8. Pin all layers (stabilizer, background, cut shapes, and tulle) together at about 6" intervals. Be sure to pin any shapes that must stay in place.

9. Prepare your sewing machine for stitching. A walking foot is the best choice at this point. Use thread to match the base fabric in the bobbin, and transparent nylon thread for the top thread. A nice combination to try is lingerie/bobbin thread in the bobbin and transparent nylon thread for the top because it creates an almost invisible sewing line, allowing the cut shapes to stand alone as the design. Reduce the top tension slightly when using transparent nylon thread, since it has a tendency to pull tightly. Try different tensions on a scrap piece of fabric to adjust it correctly.

10. For now, we will be doing a meandering straight stitch. Other styles of stitching and thread choices will be discussed later. Starting at one corner, stitch in a meandering fashion, working from the outside edges toward the center. Remove pins as you approach them. Do not stitch over them. Keep the piece as flat as possible while stitching to keep the shapes from shifting. The tear-away stabilizer will keep the piece flat so the cut pieces won't fall out. It can also act as a steering wheel to maneuver the fabric while stitching.

   How much stitching should be done? It is important to stitch down all the cut shapes or elements within the design. One line of stitching across a cut shape is enough to hold it in place if you are making a wall hanging. However, if you plan to cut up the fantasy fabric for a pieced or appliquéd project, more stitching is required. Keep in mind the sizes of the pieces to be cut from the fabric. Smaller pieces will require more stitching. Unfortunately, more stitching will make removal of the tear-away stabilizer more difficult. Specifics for piecing and appliqué are discussed in more detail later. For now, stitch the piece so each of the shapes has at least one line of stitching through them.

11. Remove the tear-away stabilizer. Pull the stabilizer against the stitching lines to free the adjacent portions of stabilizer and make it easier to remove. Use tweezers to remove any stubborn pieces of stabilizer that remain.

12. Press the fantasy fabric from the back, using a low to medium temperature setting. You now have a beautiful piece of fabric that can be used by itself or incorporated into another project.

Experimenting with Fabrics

Base Fabrics

The first question to ask yourself before you decide on a base fabric is "How will the fantasy fabric be used?" If it is going to be used in a wall hanging that will never be washed, almost any fabric is fair game. Keep in mind that you must be able to stitch and quilt through it. Think about the properties of the fabric before choosing. Is it too sheer? Is it too thick to handle and machine stitch through? Is it so thick that it will add bulk to seams if it is pieced?

Cotton, the standard for quilters, is always a good choice. It is easy to cut, stitch, and quilt. Prewash and preshrink any fabrics that will be used in a project you intend to wash. On occasion, you may find a cotton that will shrink a bit from the heat of the iron. If you don't want to prewash the fabric, use the iron to preshrink it before stitching it into a piece of fantasy fabric.

Another favorite fabric is satin. It has a beautiful luster that combines well with metallic Tintzl, metallic confetti shapes, and metallic threads. Suede cloth is another good choice for the base.

You can use stretch fabrics if you stabilize them with a lightweight fusible interfacing. Follow the manufacturer's directions for fusing the interfacing.

If you want to use tissue lamé as a base fabric, stabilize it first with a fusible woven cotton interfacing. Before applying the interfacing, preshrink the lamé by pressing with a low to medium temperature setting. It will shrink right before your eyes. *Test the temperature of the iron on a corner of the lamé before pressing the whole piece. Too much heat will melt the lamé.*

You can even use a sheer fabric for the base. A sheer base and top layer with Tintzl (page 48), silk flowers, or threads in between might make a beautiful shawl for a fancy dress. However, you'll need to choose a complementary thread for stitching the layers together, because on a sheer base fabric, the bobbin thread as well as the top thread will be visible. You'll also need to encase the raw edges of a sheer base fabric with French seams when it is used in a project.

"Genesis: A New Beginning" (page 72) incorporates pieces of black sheer base fabric. Clippings of metallic floss were captured between two layers of black tulle. Shapes were then cut from the created fabric and stitched to the surface.

The color of the base fabric will establish the overall coloration of the finished piece. The color will change somewhat, depending on what toppings are added, the color of the overlaid sheer, and the color of the top stitching thread.

The base fabric can be a solid color or a multicolor print. Toppings and a solid-color base fabric in the same color family will result in a subtle texture. A contrasting solid-color base fabric will allow the toppings to really stand out. Using a multicolor print will add yet another dimension to the overall design.

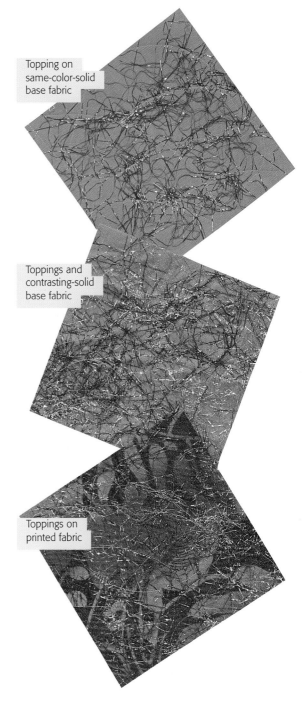

Topping on same-color-solid base fabric

Toppings and contrasting-solid base fabric

Toppings on printed fabric

A pieced background is another possibility. Judy Levine added some real excitement to her pieced background in "Emanation." The simple checkerboard background came to life when she added the cut sheer shapes.

This might be a great way to use up some of those quilt tops started in classes but never finished. One of them just might make a great base fabric for your first fantasy fabric.

Emanation (detail). Full quilt on page 21.

Top Layers

Tulle is a perfect top layer for fantasy fabric. It is very sheer and adds only a subtle color to the finished piece. Laces add their own textural quality and design element. Organza and other sheer fabrics are nice, but they filter out much of the colors and shapes captured below them. Consider using these if this is the effect you want. When selecting tulle for the top layer, consider the size of the openings in the tulle. Finer tulle and chiffon will hold smaller objects, such as glitter.

Printed sheers add another dimension to fantasy fabric. In "Sherbet Surprise," Sharon Williams used a variety of printed sheers to create a subtle design in each of the four squares so they almost look pieced.

Sherbet Surprise (detail). Full quilt on page 21.

Turquoise tulle

Black tulle with glitter

Multicolored organza

Black floral lace

Black lace netting

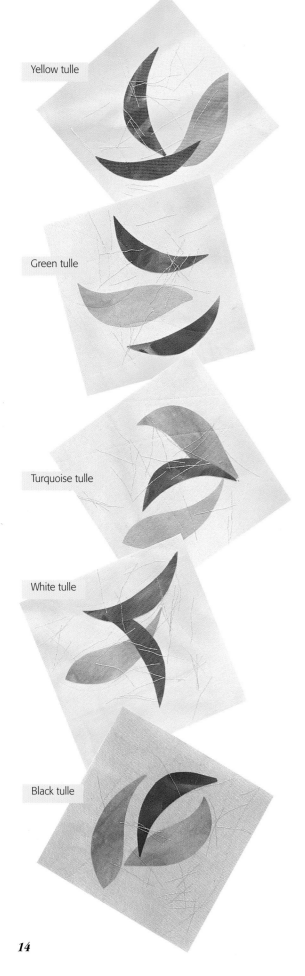

Yellow tulle

Green tulle

Turquoise tulle

White tulle

Black tulle

Determining Color Interaction

A variety of factors determines the final color of the fantasy fabric: the base fabric, the items captured, the top layer, and the color of the thread used to stitch the layers together. Try experimenting with the different elements to see what kind of results you get. Following are a few tips I've picked up along the way.

No matter what color tulle is selected, it will affect the appearance of both the base fabric and the objects captured between the layers. Matching the color of the tulle with the base fabric intensifies the color of the base fabric and slightly alters the color of the captured items. If the color of the tulle matches the captured items, the captured items will stand out more and the base fabric will be diluted. Another possibility is to find a color that is between the base fabric and the captured items. For example, if the base fabric is yellow and the captured items are turquoise, try a green tulle for the top layer. The green tulle will darken the background and lighten the captured items. Black tulle grays the colors, and white tulle adds a pastel effect.

Keep the color-mixing lessons in mind. If turquoise tulle is layered over a yellow background, the layers will definitely have a greenish tone. On the other hand, turquoise tulle layered over white silk flowers turns the flowers to a pale turquoise.

In the striped color sample, you can see how the different shades of tulle interact with the different background colors. Even the black background is affected by the various colors of tulle. The row on the far right shows the color with no top layer.

The colors in my "Bubblin' Up II" were much brighter before brown tulle was laid on top. The colors are now subtler.

Bubblin' Up II (detail.) Full quilt on page 20.

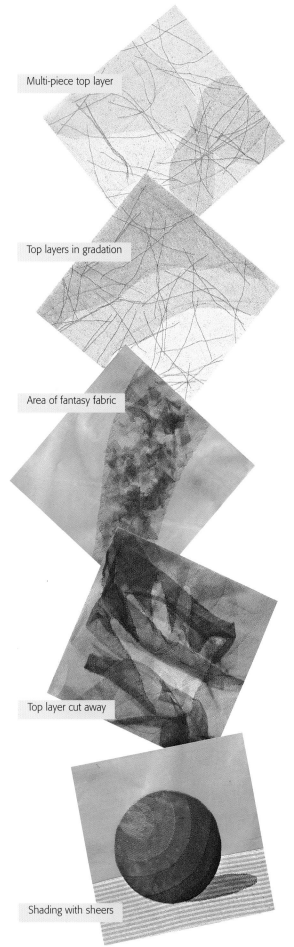

Multi-piece top layer

Top layers in gradation

Area of fantasy fabric

Top layer cut away

Shading with sheers

Using Multi-piece Top Layers

The sheer top layer does not have to be just one color. You can use pieces of different-colored tulle for the top layer, creating gradations of color or the illusion of a shaft of light. Or, you can use multiple layers of one color to intensify the color of the tulle.

When creating the gradation in the background of "Genesis: A New Beginning" (page 72), I started in one corner and added progressively larger pieces of different colored tulle, eventually covering the corner piece added at the beginning.

I used multiple layers of white and navy tulles to achieve the gradated illusion of glowing circles in "My Three Lucky Stars." The layers of white tulle grew from small areas to larger areas. Each successive layer intensified the white in the center. The navy tulle blended into the night sky.

When using multiple layers, you need to use more pins to hold the layers in place. You also need to do more stitching. Stitch carefully as you approach any cut edges to keep them from getting caught on the sewing-machine foot.

Perhaps you would like to add areas of fantasy fabric without covering the entire surface with a layer of tulle. This can be done on a plain background, or on a pieced or appliquéd design. There are two ways to mark the areas.

Draw a simple design on the base fabric with a temporary marking tool, such as the air-soluble purple pen that disappears in a matter of hours.

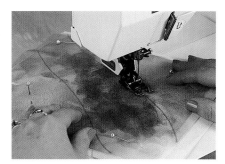

Layer the items to be captured on the base fabric within the marked area. Add a layer of tulle slightly larger than the area. Pin, then straight stitch around the edge of the design. Transparent nylon thread will allow the edge of the tulle to blend nicely into the background.

Cut away the excess tulle. Add a second row of zigzag stitching around the edge of the tulle to secure it. Add more stitching to the fantasy fabric area as needed to hold the layers and captured items in place.

If you have a more detailed shape in mind for the fantasy-fabric area, draw

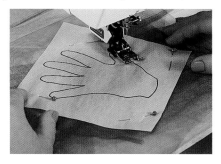

the design on tracing paper first. Prepare the area with the captured items and the top layer of tulle. Pin the tracing paper on top of the prepared area. Make sure the captured items are positioned within the design edge. Stitch through all layers, following the lines in the drawing.

Tear away the tracing paper. Use tweezers to remove any remaining fragments. Cut away the excess top layer of tulle, following the stitched line, and secure the edge with zigzag stitching.

There may be certain areas of the design where you want the brightest colors to show. Remember, the sheers dilute whatever colors are layered underneath them. You can remove a portion of the top layer of sheer, but keep in mind that whatever was captured under the layer will need to be secured. Layer captured items so that they touch at least two edges of the opening. This will keep the items in place as you stitch the opening. Stitch the edge of the area to be cut away. Trim away the interior area of the tulle, being careful not to cut the captured items. Reinforce the sheer cut edge with zigzag stitching, and add stitching over the captured items to further secure them. In the sample with the top layer cut away, the hand shape cut from the top layer of tulle reveals the captured items.

The wonderful transparent quality of sheer fabrics makes them perfect for modifying the underlying colors ever so slightly. Use yellows and whites for highlights, and navies, purples, and blacks for shadows. Multiple layers of a dark tulle will darken the underlying fabric even more. In the bottom sample on the facing page, the shading in the ball was achieved by first stitching the smallest shapes. The largest pieces of tulle were added last to control the edges of the small pieces.

Cutting Accurate Sheer Shapes

Cutting a specific shape from sheer fabrics can be tricky, since they usually have more bounce and spunk than cotton fabrics. The most accurate way to cut single layers is to use freezer-paper templates.

1. Trace the design onto the uncoated side of freezer paper.
2. Iron the freezer-paper pattern to the tulle, using a dry iron on a medium temperature setting. The freezer paper will hold the tulle in place while you are cutting.
3. Cut out the shape with sharp scissors or a rotary cutter (depending on the intricacy of the design).
4. Carefully peel the freezer-paper template from the cut piece. Iron this pattern onto another piece of tulle to cut additional pieces.

TIP

Freezer-paper patterns can be reused several times. When a pattern is just starting to lose its "stickiness," iron it to another piece of freezer paper before ironing it to the tulle. As you cut the tulle shape, you will cut a new freezer-paper template.

My Three Lucky Stars (detail.) Full quilt on page 20.

Scrunched blue tulle

Scrunched blue and green tulle

Scrunched white tulle with pearls added

Scrunched yellow tulle over multicolored tulle snips

Scrunching Sheers

Another elegant effect can be achieved by "scrunching" the top layer of sheer fabric.

1. Cut the top layer about 1½ to 2 times the length and width of the base fabric. Pin the corners of the sheer fabric to the corners of the base fabric.

2. Loosely pinch or scrunch the excess fabric and pin in place.

3. Stitch the scrunched sheer down. A word of caution here: The sewing-machine foot has a tendency to get caught in the folds of the sheer. Work slowly, pressing the folds flat while guiding them under the foot. If the foot gets caught in the folds, carefully snip the sheer free from the foot.

One way to avoid getting the folds caught in the sewing machine foot is to top the entire piece with another layer of flat tulle. This will, however, change the color of the layers.

Another possibility is to combine layers of different-colored scrunched fabrics. The colors will interact with each other, creating new colors where they overlap.

Sheer fabrics can also be folded and manipulated in a systematic way, such as pleating, tucking, or fan folding. Chiffon was carefully folded into a soft fan shape in "Genesis."

Adding pearls to the scrunched fabric also creates a stunning effect. Depending on how the adorned fabric will be used, it is usually best to add the pearls after the fabric has been incorporated into a piece.

Genesis by Laurie D Calvitti, 1998, Hawley, Pennsylvania, 21½" x 25½". "This piece speaks of new life—in the primordial waters and as a new beginning in my own creative life. It throws off sparks in many directions. Thanks to Bonnie's class, I've learned to take chances and 'just do it'!"

My Three Lucky Stars (above) by Bonnie Lyn McCaffery, 1998, Hawley, Pennsylvania, 27" x 18". Multiple layers of navy and white tulle are layered to create a starry night. Creative Crystals rhinestones in different sizes sparkle in the night sky.

Bubblin' Up II (right) by Bonnie Lyn McCaffery, 1998, Hawley, Pennsylvania, 43" x 48". Various sheer fabrics cut into teardrops, moon slivers, and other shapes are muted by the brown tulle covering them. Metallic and silver thread is drizzled on the surface, and beads add interest.

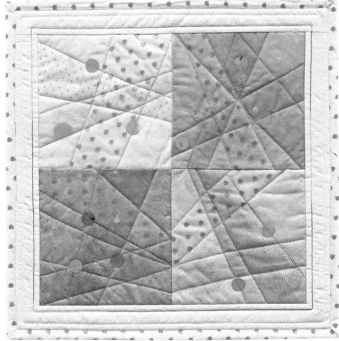

Emanation (above) by Judy Zoelzer Levine, 1997, Bayside, Wisconsin, 72" x 60½". Hand-dyed fabrics in a gradation of pinks, purples, and grays form the background of this quilt. Tulle is layered from one to three thicknesses to produce depth. Pearlized white and glitter paints add accents.

Sherbet Surprise (left) by Sharon Lee Williams, 1998, Matamoras, Pennsylvania, 19½" x 19½". Tulle with different-sized holes and textured tulle are layered over sequins. The binding is also a fabric covered by textured tulle.

Stitching the Layers Together

Thread Choices

Stitching the layers together can be done with a variety of threads. Transparent nylon thread is almost invisible, allowing the shapes and captured items to stand alone as the design. Clear and a smoke color are available. Use the smoke-colored thread on darker fabrics. Loosen the top tension on the sewing machine when you use transparent nylon thread.

Using colored threads to stitch the layers together will add another element to the design. You can match the thread to the color of the shapes or the base fabric, or use a contrasting color to add another aspect to the design. Rayon threads have a lovely luster; metallic threads add wonderful sparkle. Whenever metallic threads are loaded into the top of the machine, use a needle made for metallic threads (such as a Metallica or Metafil), and loosen the top tension to reduce thread breakage. Having to stop and rethread can be very annoying.

Stitching Styles

A variety of styles can be used to stitch the layers together. Refer to some of the great machine-quilting books for styles not discussed here. Many of these styles can be done with straight stitching, zigzag, or decorative stitches.

Various ribbons, braids, and trims can be couched with transparent nylon thread or a contrasting-color thread. A braiding foot or piping foot helps accommodate the bulk of the trims and braids.

Use a walking foot for straight-line stitching or gentle curves to help feed the layers evenly, giving you the most consistent lines. If the design requires a lot of turning, use a darning foot, lower the feed dogs, and stitch in free motion.

Free-motion stitching is not appropriate for programmed decorative stitching. Use it for stitching curved lines and free-form designs. Mastering free-motion stitching is a matter of practice. Practice on a piece of copier paper with the needle unthreaded to get the feel of the motion.

To get started, hold the top thread and take one stitch to pull the bobbin thread to the top. Don't forget to lower the presser foot. Hold both threads out of the way and stitch in place a few times to lock the thread ends. Begin stitching while moving the fabric with your hands. Cut the thread tails after a few stitches, when they are free from the presser foot.

When the feed dogs are down, you must keep the fabric moving or the stitches will pile up in one place. Stitch at a fairly fast speed to get the stitches close enough together. Stitches that are too long will distort and pull apart when the stabilizer is removed. If you need to stop to reposition the fabric, stop moving your hands just before stopping the machine. Then when you are ready to go again, start the machine and then your hand motion.

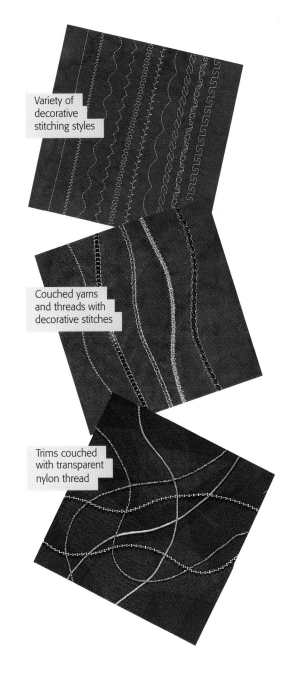

Variety of decorative stitching styles

Couched yarns and threads with decorative stitches

Trims couched with transparent nylon thread

Braiding foot

Piping foot — Groove

Walking foot

Darning foot

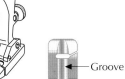

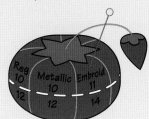

TIP

To keep track of sewing machine needles, use a tomato pincushion. Mark each section of the pincushion with a permanent pen, indicating the different types of needles such as:

Regular (size 10 or 12),
Metallic (size 10 or 12),
Embroidery (size 11 or 14),

As you put a specific type of needle into the sewing machine, place a colored pin into that section of the pincushion. Move the pin to the appropriate section of the pincushion each time the needle is changed.

The pin means you have an Embroidery needle, size 11, in the machine.

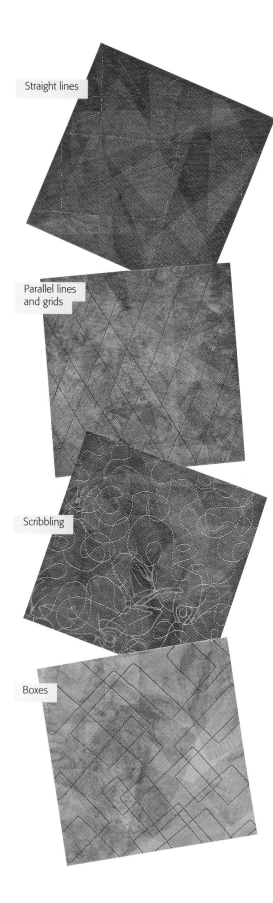

Straight lines

Parallel lines and grids

Scribbling

Boxes

Stitching Designs

Each of the twelve stitching samples on these pages was done using only seven fabrics so you can see how the base fabrics are affected by the color of the tulle on top. Can you pick out the pieces that share a base fabric? (Answer: straight lines and loops, boxes and echoing, gentle curves and leaves, parallel lines and drawing, wandering stars and stippling. Scribbling and swirls *do not* have the same base fabric.)

Straight Lines

Use a walking foot or regular sewing-machine foot. You can stitch straight lines from edge to edge, changing directions every time you get to the edge. Or, you can stitch random straight lines within the piece, without going to the edge every time you make a turn. As the lines develop, you will be able to see areas that need more stitching.

Parallel Lines and Grids

An old standby method of parallel lines or grids is an easy way to fill an area and hold the layers together. The grid can be done at right angles, 30° or 60° angles, or any other angle. Start by stitching an X at the desired angles. Then use the legs of the X as guides to stitch parallel lines that will form the grid. For a dense fill, stitch lines at ¼" intervals. Use wider intervals for a looser grid. Another possibility is to stitch parallel lines at varying intervals.

Scribbling

An easy way to hold the layers together is to just scribble in a free-form design. This is a good style to start with if you have never done free-motion stitching.

Boxes

Just a slight modification to the straight-line stitching results in Art Deco–style boxes. While stitching, rotate the fabric at right angles to form a box. Then continue stitching to another area to start another box. To make sharp corners, stop the machine with the needle in the down position. Notice in the sample that the stitched boxes mimic the square pieces of tulle. Use a walking foot or regular sewing-machine foot for this technique. You can vary the design further by stitching diamonds or triangles instead of squares.

Gentle Curves

Gentle curves are a lovely way to fill an area. Stitch a gentle curve for awhile, then change direction, curving in another direction.

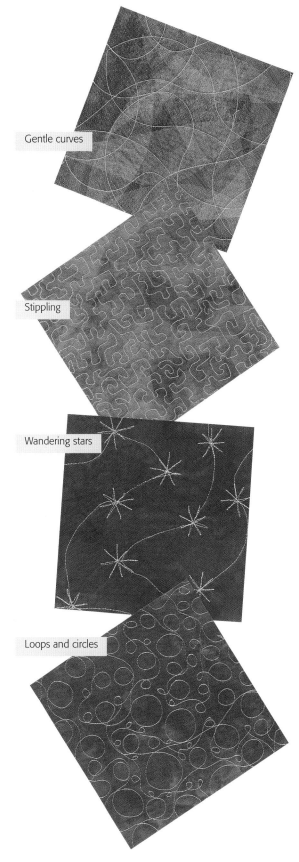

> ### TIP
>
> A great way to create these gentle curves is to use your finger as a pivot point. Decide how tight you want the curve to be. If the pivot point is close to the needle, it will form a tight curve. A pivot point farther from the needle will create a looser curve. The pivot point can be to the left or the right of the needle. Switching from one side to the other will create a gentle S curve. Gently press down on the pivot point with your finger and let the feed dogs do the work.
>
>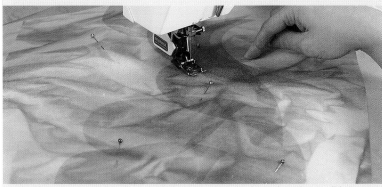
>
> Gentle curves can be done with free-motion stitching, but they will be easier to control with a walking foot.

Stippling

Another favorite way to fill an area is stippling. In this free-motion technique, the stitching lines do not cross each other, and the direction of the stitching changes often. Vary the density and size of the stippling pattern to create different effects. Denser and smaller stippling will reflect more of the thread color. Looser and larger stippling will show more of the stippling design and allow the background to show through.

Wandering Stars

The stitching that holds the layers together can be unobtrusive, or stand out and be a design by itself. In the sample, the stars were connected with lines of stitching, but they could have been done individually by lifting the presser foot and moving to the next star. Lock the stitches at the beginning and end of each star, and trim the connecting threads between the stars. Try stitching five-pointed stars—the kind we made as kids. For very large stars, you can use a walking foot or regular sewing-machine foot. For smaller stars, it's easier to use a darning foot and free-motion stitching.

Loops and Circles

Loops are just elongated circles. The loops and circles in the sample were done in various sizes, but they could have been done all the same size. Notice how the circles change direction from one to the next, first clockwise and then counterclockwise. As you make each circle or loop, think about where to place the next one. This will help the lines flow smoothly. Try converting the circles or loops to hearts. Use a darning foot and free-motion stitching.

Gentle curves

Stippling

Wandering stars

Loops and circles

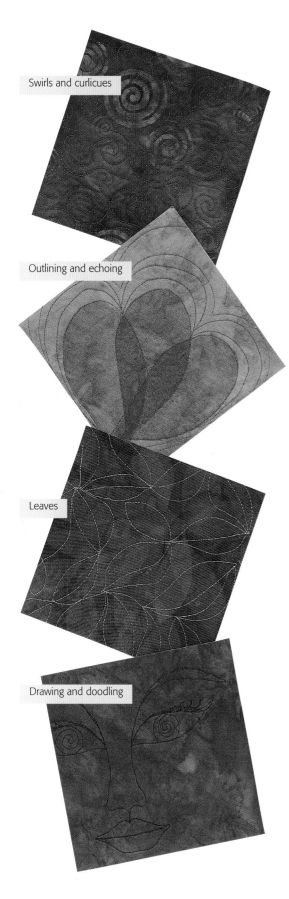

Swirls and curlicues

Outlining and echoing

Leaves

Drawing and doodling

Swirls and Curlicues

Swirls and curlicues take more control to draw with the sewing-machine needle. Curve to the inside and then follow the line back to the outside while traveling to the place where the next swirl will begin. Take a couple stitches at the "point" of the curlicue before changing direction. If you need to stop and reposition your hands, do this at the point. You can vary the size of the swirls and curlicue, depending on the desired look. Use a darning foot and free-motion stitching.

Outlining and Echoing

If you want the cut sheer shapes to stand out, outline them with a line of stitching. Be careful with some of the fabrics that fray (see page 28). Stitching on the edge of some fabrics will make them fray more, so stitch outside the edges of these fabrics. You can stitch on the edge of fabrics that do not fray, such as tulle. Use a darning foot or free-motion foot if there are a lot of twists and turns in the design.

Echoing the shape (outlining with three or four parallel lines) will emphasize its design. This can be done tightly and accurately or loosely.

Leaves

Leaves can be stitched in a continuous motion so the end of one leaf is the beginning of the next leaf. Decide whether or not to add a vein, depending on where you want the next leaf to start. A vein is a perfect way to travel to the other end of the leaf. These are simple leaves, but there is a great variety of leaves, from simple to complex. Why not try an oak, a maple, or a long, thin leaf? Practice drawing more leaves on paper to get into the flow of stitching a leaf shape. Use a darning foot and free-motion stitching.

Drawing and Doodling

Coloring books offer some wonderful line drawings. Or, perhaps you like to sketch. Refine your sketch to a line drawing that can be stitched on fabric.

If your drawing is simple enough, you can stitch the design directly onto the fabric. For more complex drawings, trace the design on tracing paper with a permanent pen. Pin the paper in place, stitch on the drawn lines, then remove the paper.

Analyze the drawing to see if you can stitch it in one continuous motion or if you have to stop and move the needle. Be sure to lock the stitches at the beginning and end of each line.

Another way to draw on fabric is to trace the design on the wrong side of the fabric, then stitch from the back. Whatever thread you used in the bobbin will appear on the front of the fabric.

Doodling on fabric is just as easy. Simply sketch with your needle as you move the fabric. Free-motion stitching is the best way to draw or doodle on fabric.

Adding Captured Items

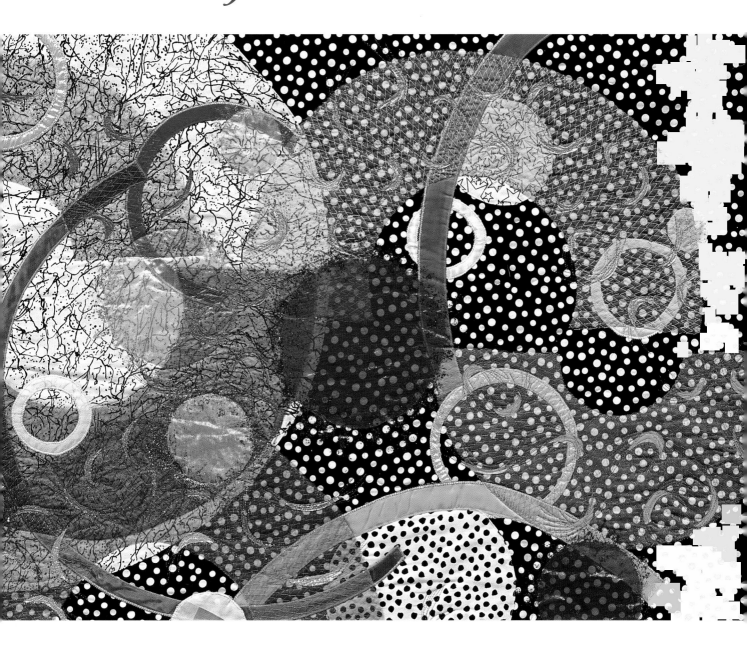

Straight strips

Wavy strips

Randomly placed
curved strips

Fabrics

Choices of fabrics you can capture are endless. In addition to a variety of sheer fabrics, you can use cottons, suede cloth, felt, vinyl, fake fur, velour, velvet, leather—just about any fabric you wish.

I found some interesting fabrics called Abaca Fibre, Pulp Netting, and Banana Wrap in a catalog containing handmade papers (see "Loose Ends" in the resources). These fibers give a natural, rustic appearance to my quilt "It's Only Natural."

Look at the fabrics carefully to determine whether the edges are likely to fray when cut. This can affect the outcome of your fantasy fabric. Some fabrics do not fray at all, like tricot lamé, Ultra Suede, suede cloth, felt, and netting. You can easily cut these without the edges fraying. Other fabrics will hold their cut edge well, like cottons, polyesters, tricot, blends, vinyl, and leather.

If you choose a fabric that has a tendency to fray, you have two options: you can accept the fraying and deal with it as described in "Torn Scraps" on page 32, or you can do something about it.

Fabrics like tissue lamé, organza, and linen fray easily when cut. Stabilize opaque fabrics by fusing them to a lightweight interfacing. Remember to be careful when pressing tissue lamés. They tend to shrink with heat (see page 11).

You can stabilize sheer fabrics by fusing them to a fusible web. This will reduce the transparent effect of the fabric and make the fabrics a little stiffer, so try a sample before resorting to fusible web.

See "Outlining and Echoing" on page 26 for information about stitching around fabrics that fray.

Strips

Strips of colored sheers can be arranged to create a striped design or woven to create a plaid effect. New colors are created where the strips overlap.

Rather than straight-edge strips, try wavy-edged strips. Varying the widths of the strips will also create a very different look.

It's Only Natural (detail). Full quilt on page 35.

Cut Shapes

The possibilities for cut shapes are endless. Try cutting squares, circles, triangles, teardrops, moon slivers, and even following existing designs in a fabric. While all these shapes can be cut with a straight-edge rotary blade, why not try some of the interesting blades developed by Fiskars? Pinking, Squiggle, Wave, Victorian, Deckle, Scallop, and Tiara are just some of the blades they make. These will add texture to the cut edges of any fabrics.

I created the initial practice piece by cutting organic shapes from sheer fabrics and placing them on a single base fabric. You can also capture sheer shapes on appliquéd and pieced quilt tops to add further interest and texture. Notice how Judy Levine used sheer circles and half circles to create a three-dimensional look in her quilt, "She Dreams in Color."

You can also use precut felt shapes, which are available in a variety of designs. Since the cutting is already done, these are great to use when you need a quick project.

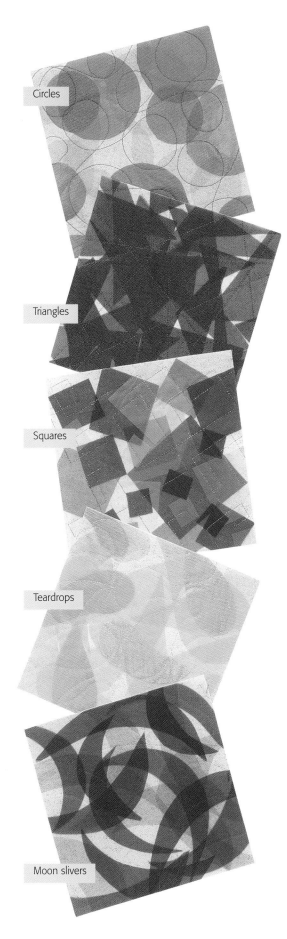

Circles

Triangles

Squares

Teardrops

Moon slivers

She Dreams in Color (detail). Full quilt on page 38.

Other Cuts

Shapes can be cut from a printed fabric without following the design in the fabric.

I cut the leaf and petal shapes in "My Secret Sister's Fantasy" randomly from a printed fabric. My secret sister had given me some wonderful fabrics throughout the year, and I wanted her to see that I was enjoying them, so I incorporated them into this piece.

Random cuts from printed fabric

Specific cuts for color

Cuts from novelty print

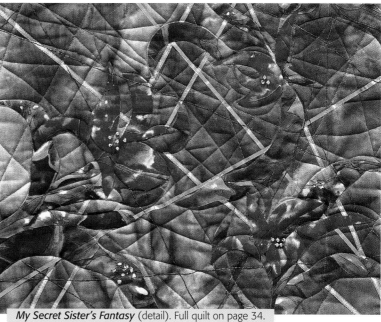

My Secret Sister's Fantasy (detail). Full quilt on page 34.

You can also cut specific areas in a fabric to take advantage of a particular color. The light and dark areas in the tulip design were cut from a fabric featuring mouth-watering oranges. You will view printed fabrics in a whole new light once you think of printed designs as areas of color and not as designs that represent something.

The novelty prints available today are another source for great designs. You can find just about any flower, critter, or object on a printed fabric. Use small, sharp scissors to cut intricate shapes. The cats in the print at right were carefully cut and arranged to look like a "Meow" family portrait captured by a photographer.

You can create a beautiful flower garden or bouquet by cutting flowers from a variety of floral prints. Or, perhaps you would like a little frog sitting on a lily pad. The possibilities for using novelty prints are endless.

Linda Poole cut angels and a sun to add a heavenly touch to "Where Angels Play." In "Catching Some Rays," Linda cut a variety of fish, scuba divers, and dolphins from several different prints to create a wonderful underwater scene.

Where Angels Play (detail). Full quilt on page 37.

Catching Some Rays (detail). Full quilt on page 39.

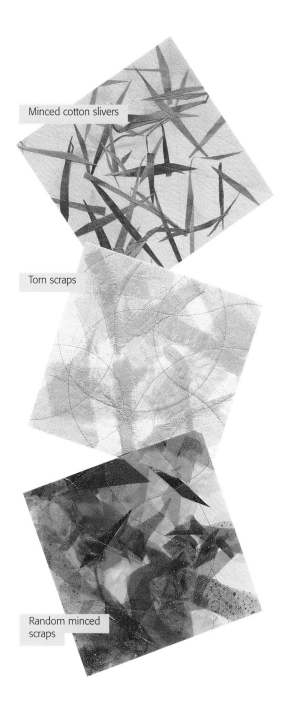

Minced cotton slivers

Torn scraps

Random minced scraps

Torn, Minced, and Distorted Fabrics

Torn Scraps

If you want to use fabrics that have a tendency to fray, why not use this quality to add visual texture. Torn edges give a contemporary flair to a design. Tear the pieces to get a thready appearance. Snip the edges to start the tear. When positioning the pieces, allow the frayed threads to fall naturally in place. Don't trim them away. Most woven fabrics will only tear on the straight grain so the shapes will have a linear quality. You can pull and distort the pieces to achieve a more relaxed design.

Tulle and other fabrics that do not fray can also be torn and distorted into interesting shapes. Experiment. Try pulling on opposite corners of tulle pieces.

Minced Scraps

Slivered cotton pieces add a wonderful texture to any fantasy fabric. To make the slivers, cut back and forth with a rotary cutter, curving ever so slightly. Cut carefully and keep fingers out of the way. Sprinkle these on a background and cover with a layer of tulle. I used just one color to do the sample, but imagine the beauty of many colors or possibly different-sized slivers. Remember to use enough stitching to hold all the tiny slivers in place.

As you create fantasy fabrics, you will end up with some wonderful scraps. Save all of these, no matter how small. I have a glass candy jar on my sewing table where I collect all sorts of interesting pieces, in-cluding sheer fabrics, metal-lic threads, Tintzl, and anything else that might be usable. As Helen Marinaro says, "Nothing goes to waste." Helen made "Tangel" (page 46) from a variety of scraps and leftovers.

To mince a pile of sheer fabric scraps, run the rotary cutter back and forth over the pieces. Use a rotary ruler to hold the pieces in place. This is safer than cutting freely without the ruler. Keep cutting until you get the desired-size pieces.

Arrange the minced scraps on a base fabric that is supported by a tear-away stabilizer. At this point, you can add more interest and fun by sprinkling confetti, glitter, and Tintzl. Add the top layer of tulle. Smooth the layers as flat as possible. Use as many pins as needed to hold the layers together. Stitch the layers together in a design of your choice. Remember that the smaller the pieces are, the more stitching you'll have to do.

While creating "If I Could Touch Heaven I," I saved all of the scraps. Then I went back and made a second version using the leftover scraps, which I minced. I added a few confetti stars to complete "If I Could Touch Heaven II."

If I Could Touch Heaven I (detail). Full quilt on page 36.

If I Could Touch Heaven II (detail). Full quilt on page 36.

My Secret Sister's Fantasy by Bonnie Lyn McCaffery, 1998, Hawley, Pennsylvania, 23" x 27". Cut areas of colored fabric, gold ribbons, and threads are captured on a background of hand-painted fabric.

It's Only Natural by Bonnie Lyn McCaffery, 1998, Hawley, Pennsylvania, 25" x 28". Flowers, Abaca Fibre, Pulp Netting, Banana, and strips of painted corrugated cardboard from Loose Ends have been capture under a layer of tulle.

If I Could Touch Heaven I (above) by Bonnie Lyn McCaffery, 1998, Hawley, Pennsylvania, 18" x 24". Various cut sheers and drizzled gold thread were used in this simple piece.

If I Could Touch Heaven II (right) by Bonnie Lyn McCaffery, 1998, Hawley, Pennsylvania, 18" x 26". Minced scraps from "If I Could Touch Heaven I" were combined with metallic stars in this second fantasy fabric piece.

Where Angels Play by Linda M. Poole, 1998, Milford, Pennsylvania, 20" x 25". Minced scraps of various fabrics, shredded mylar, metallic-confetti shapes, feathers, cut angels, and a sun are incorporated into a fun piece of fantasy fabric.

She Dreams in Color (above) by Judy Zoelzer Levine, 1995, Bayside, Wisconsin, 52½" x 61". Organza and tulle half-circles are zigzagged to the surface with matching thread. Iridescent poly-sheer circles are appliquéd on top. Satin rings and half-rings complete the picture.

Catching Some Rays (right) by Linda M. Poole, 1998, Milford, Pennsylvania, 18" x 27". Stingrays, scuba divers, and fish are captured along with metallic confetti, ribbons, and Jimmies in this underwater piece. Lots of sculptured embellishments, buttons, and beads add a textural element to the bottom of the sea. Even a treasured button from grand aunt Tante Alice has been included.

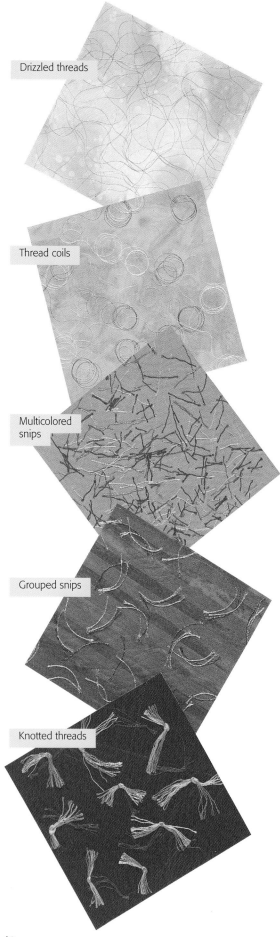

Drizzled threads

Thread coils

Multicolored snips

Grouped snips

Knotted threads

Threads

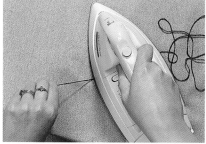

An endless variety of threads and embroidery floss can be used in fantasy fabrics. These are available in cotton, rayon, silk, synthetic, and metallic. Most threads are wound on spools, while embroidery floss comes in skeins.

Spooled threads will have no kinks in them. But skeins of floss might need to be straightened with an iron. Pull the length you expect to use out of the skein before starting to iron it. Set the iron to a medium temperature. Always do a test on one end to be sure the thread will not melt or burn. Place the iron on one end of the thread, with a tail sticking out. Gently pull the thread under the iron. If an iron is not available, pull the threads through wet fingertips to straighten the kinks.

There are a number of techniques for adding threads to a base fabric to create fantasy fabrics. You can use them alone or in conjunction with other captured items. "YLI's Fantasy Thread Sampler" (page 47) incorporates several of the techniques using threads and ribbons. A sampler is a great way to experiment and have fun trying several techniques.

Drizzled Threads

Thread or floss can be gracefully laid over the base fabric, allowing the thread to fall where it will. Drizzling can be done with any of the threads, yarns, flosses, ribbons, or braids.

Helen Marinaro had some beautiful gold Kreinik Japan thread, but it became tangled. Since it was difficult to untangle, she used it as an area of color along with some feathers and stars in "Tangel" at right.

Thread Coils

An interesting effect can be achieved by letting thread fall from the end of a spool into coils and circles. Hold the spool perpendicular to the background fabric. Some threads will fall easily off the end of the spool. Others will need to be gently pulled off the spool. To form tight circles, hold the spool close to the surface. If you get loops instead of circles, you can sometimes gently coax the loops into circles. Try using a variegated thread to add a variety of colors.

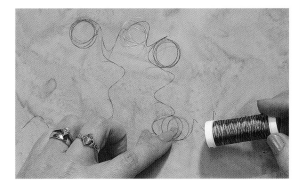

Random Snips

Any of the threads, floss, or trims can be snipped and allowed to fall randomly. The length of the snips is up to you. Short snips will have lots of texture. Longer snips will have more structure.

Multicolored Snips

Group different-colored threads and snip them at the same time to ensure that there is an equal distribution of the combined colors. Of course, you can add a larger concentration of one color to offset this balance of color if desired. Hold the threads about 6" to 8" above the surface while cutting them so that they will fall in a random pattern.

Floss comes in a variety of plies. Use a six-ply floss as is to form a heavier line, or separate the plies after they have been snipped and are on the surface. Grouping two or three colors of rayon or metallic embroidery floss creates a pretty effect. Cut the grouped threads in ½" lengths. Let them fall randomly on the surface, then work them with your fingertips to separate the plies. A variation might be to cut irregular lengths of threads.

Tangel (detail). Full quilt on page 46.

Knotted Threads

Another design option is to use bundles of knotted thread. Iron the floss or thread if there are kinks. Tie simple knots at 1" or 2" intervals along the length of floss or thread. I find it is easier to tie a number of knots rather than tying and cutting each knot individually. Cut between the knots, so each knot has two tails. Trim the tails as desired. Place knots closer or farther apart for different effects.

Try knotting two or more colors of thread or floss. Or, combine threads, floss, ribbons, yarns, and trims into knotted bundles. Oh, the marvelous possibilities!

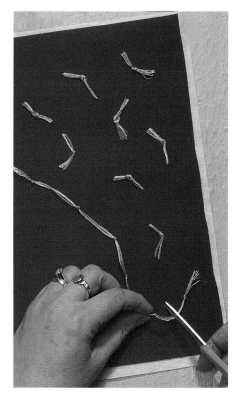

Grouped Snips

Cutting a group of threads close to the surface (1" to 3" above the surface) creates a nice pattern. This allows the threads to fall close together, forming a repeat pattern as they are clipped in different areas of the piece. Try to get the threads to curve in the same direction.

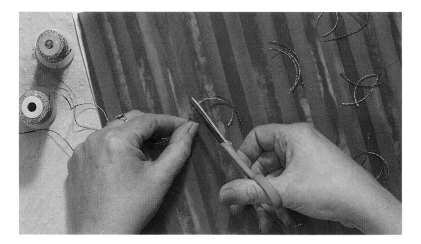

YLI's Fantasy Thread Sampler (detail). Full quilt on page 47.

Ribbons

Ribbons can be snipped, drizzled, and knotted as described in the "Threads" section. Satin, woven, metallic, silk, silk organdy, and gift ribbons are all possibilities. You can use wired-edge ribbons by removing the wire. Sheer ribbons are beautiful to use because the colors will interact with each other as they travel around the piece.

Each of the ribbon samples started with a white background fabric. Notice how the color of the piece changes as different-colored pieces of tulle are placed on top.

Caution: Whenever you use unusual ribbons, like the holographic or gift ribbons, test the effect of the iron before using the ribbon. Ironing holographic or metallic ribbons will sometimes dull them. If that is the case, iron the fabric before starting, and limit future ironing when using this type of trim. You might be able to iron carefully around the ribbon, avoiding contact with the holographic ribbon. Sometimes it is worth the extra effort to be able to incorporate such an interesting ribbon.

Ribbon Snips

A nice texture is achieved by combining different-width snips of satin ribbons. Cutting the wider ribbon at an angle gives the design another element of interest. Try cutting ribbons in a variety of lengths.

Twisted Ribbons

A wonderful quality of ribbon is how beautiful it looks when it is twisted and turned. Wider ribbons will show off the twists better than narrow ribbons. If the ribbon has a mind of its own and won't stay twisted, pin the fold with regular, small-headed straight pins. The heads of these pins will pop through the tulle for easy removal.

Drizzled Ribbons

Ribbons can be randomly "drizzled" on a background. Or, they can be positioned in a loose striped effect. Since ribbons are flat, there will be a twist every time they change direction. These twists add another interesting element. The endless variety of color, width, and types of ribbon give texture and interest to a design.

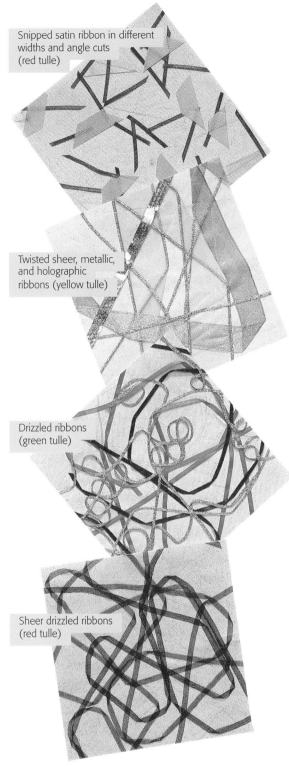

Snipped satin ribbon in different widths and angle cuts (red tulle)

Twisted sheer, metallic, and holographic ribbons (yellow tulle)

Drizzled ribbons (green tulle)

Sheer drizzled ribbons (red tulle)

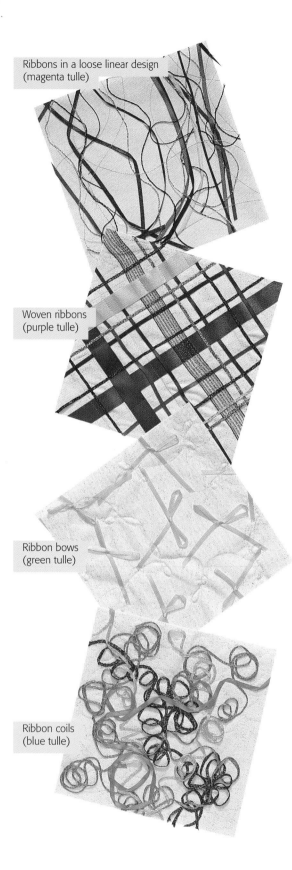

Ribbons in a loose linear design (magenta tulle)

Woven ribbons (purple tulle)

Ribbon bows (green tulle)

Ribbon coils (blue tulle)

Woven Ribbons

Ribbons can be arranged in straight lines as in the woven sample. To keep the ribbons in place until they are stitched, pin the ends with standard small-headed pins or apply a dab of glue from a temporary fabric gluestick. Let the glue dry before stitching or avoid stitching the glued ends. You do not want the glue to come in contact with the sewing machine.

Another possibility is to use a "pinnable" cardboard base to hold the ribbons in place until the tulle is positioned and pinned. Place the cardboard under the stabilizer. Pin the edges of the ribbon into the cardboard. Remove the pins from the cardboard once the top layer has been added and the ribbon ends have been secured with pins.

Ribbon Bows

Little ribbon bows are another possibility. You can make bows with one color of ribbon or group several colors together for a multicolored appearance. It is easier to tie several bows on one piece of ribbon before cutting them apart.

Ribbon Coils

Some ⅛"-wide metallic ribbons are wound on spools. You can let the ribbon fall off the spool into coils as described in "Thread Coils" (page 41), or you can coil the ribbon on a pencil. Narrow ribbons will coil better than wider ribbons. Wind a length of thin satin ribbon around a pencil, spray with starch, and let dry.

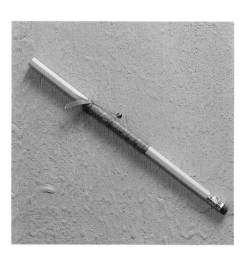

Yarns and Strings

Yarns and strings will add another dimension to your fantasy fabric. There are chenille yarns, fuzzy yarns, nubby yarns, and sparkly yarns. Check out knitting, embroidery, and weaving shops to find plenty of possibilities. If the yarn has kinks or undesirable bends, straighten these with an iron. Be sure to test the temperature, since many yarns may contain manmade fibers that are sensitive to heat.

Yarns are heavier than most threads and will show up well on a base fabric. Like threads and ribbons, yarns can also be snipped, drizzled, or arranged in lines and grids.

To create a grid, pin or glue the ends of the yarn to hold them in place. Layer with tulle and stitch. Be sure to let the glue dry or don't stitch the glued areas, to protect your machine.

While shopping in a Wal-Mart, I found a package of neon string. I drizzled the string in a color progression across a black base fabric to make "No Strings Attached." You never know where you will find things to use in fantasy fabric.

Variety of textured yarns drizzled

Random yarn snips

Yarn snips in color patterns

Stripes using various yarns

Structured grid

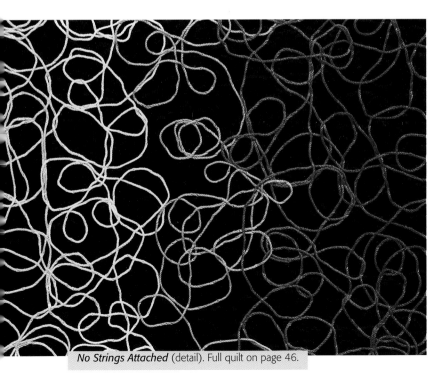

No Strings Attached (detail). Full quilt on page 46.

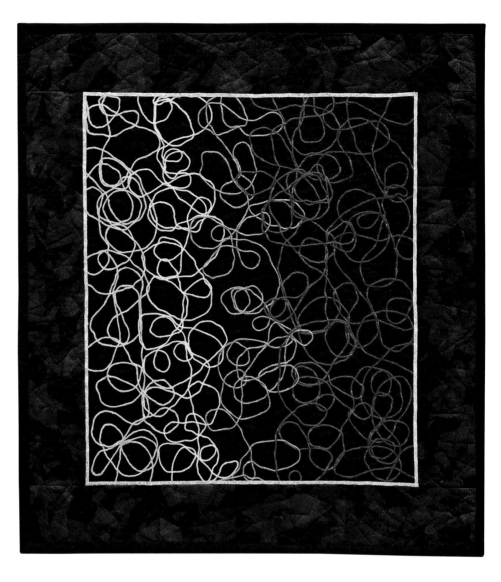

No Strings Attached (above)
by Bonnie Lyn McCaffery,1998,
Hawley, Pennsylvania, 24" x 27".
Neon strings are simply captured
under a layer of tulle.

Tangel (right) by Helen P. Marinaro,
1998, Sparrowbush, New York,
13½" x 13½". Kreinik Japan thread,
feathers, and gold stars are used in
this experimental piece.

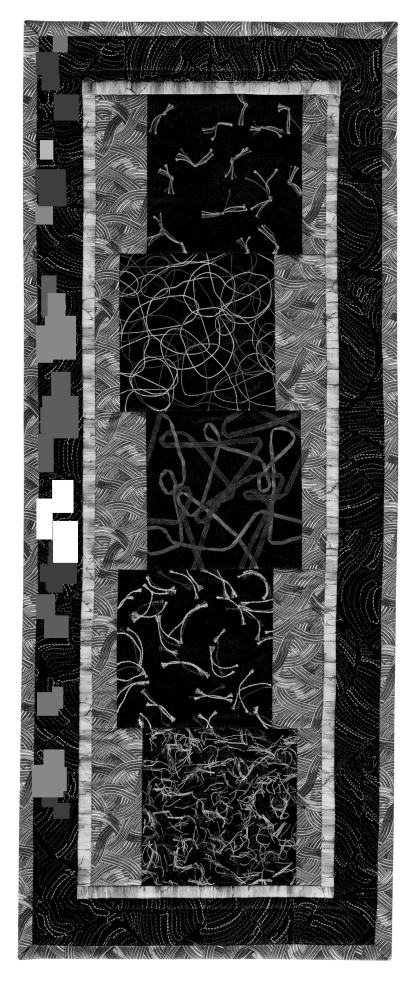

YLI's Fantasy Thread Sampler by Bonnie Lyn McCaffery, 1998, Hawley, Pennsylvania, 14" x 35". Various YLI threads and ribbons are used in this sampler to show some of the different uses for their threads. Blocks include tied snips, drizzled thread, drizzled ribbon, grouped snips, and multicolored snips.

Diagonal gold trims topped with gold tulle

Lace trims in gentle curves, topped with magenta tulle

Snipped trims, topped with black tulle

Lace motifs, topped with yellow tulle

Motifs cut and repositioned, topped with green tulle

Trims and Laces

Beautiful trims and laces can be captured in fantasy fabrics, and you can use these in many ways, similar to ribbons. All of the samples were created using the same green base fabric, but were topped with different colors of tulle. Notice again how the top layer of tulle affects the overall appearance.

Arrange lines of trim or lace diagonally or in graceful curves. Keep lines straight or allow them to cross each other.

Just as threads and yarns can be snipped and sprinkled on a surface, so can trims. Keep in mind that trims will sometimes unravel a little when they are cut. Let this be part of the design, or search for trims that unravel very little when cut. Apply Fray Check to the cut ends of trims that do unravel; let dry.

Laces come in a variety of sizes, and many are available as individual motifs. Some motifs come attached on a string. Cut out motifs or sections of lace as desired and arrange them into a design. Or, cut apart motifs and segments of trim and arrange the parts to form a new motif. Notice the two motifs in the bottom sample. Both use the same parts of a lace design, but they are arranged differently.

Take a stroll down the trim aisle at your favorite craft or fabric store and let your creativity run wild.

Sparkly Stuff

Tintzl

If you haven't already discovered this wonderful product by Jimmy Jems, you're in for a pleasant surprise. Tintzl is similar to the tinsel used on Christmas trees, but is finer and comes in a lovely array of colors. It adds extra sparkle and light to fantasy fabric and is easy to use. It is definitely one of my favorite additions to

fantasy fabric. Simply cut open a corner of the package, pull out a few strands at a time, and lay them on the base fabric. Use it in conjunction with any of the other techniques to add sparkle and make a piece glisten.

You can use Tintzl colors individually to create separate areas of color or combine colors to create multi-color areas. Notice how Laurie Calvetti used different colors of Tintzl to create an area that sparkles in the right-hand square of "Dancing on the Delaware."

Let the Tintzl fall randomly or comb it into a linear design. Use a hair pick to comb the fibers while holding the ends with your other hand.

You can also gently coerce Tintzl into loose shapes. When stitching the layers together, repeat the shape with similar stitching. This will not only clarify the shape but also hold the Tintzl in place.

Use it on a solid or printed background. When used by itself on a background, Tintzl makes a beautiful piece of fantasy fabric, which can be incorporated into a project or stand alone as an abstract piece. "Cosmic Energy" is an example of the type of wonderful design you can create using only Tintzl between the base fabric and the tulle.

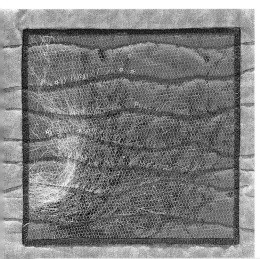

Dancing on the Delaware (detail). Four colors of Tintzl are shaped into a design. Full quilt on page 73.

Caution: Some Tintzls will melt with the heat of an iron. Iridescent and translucent Tintzls are more likely to melt, while metallic Tintzls do not. Test prior to pressing the finished piece. Either use a medium-temperature iron protected by a piece of typing or copier paper, or do not press at all.

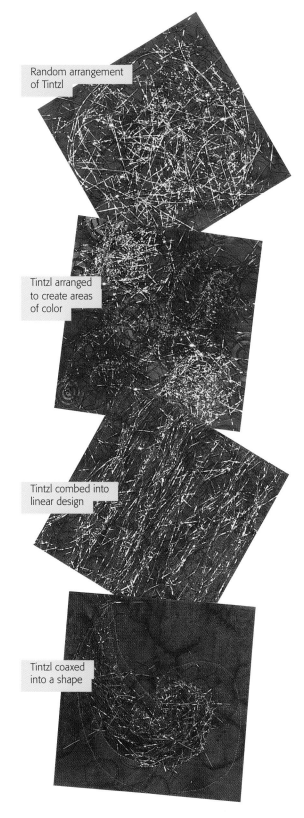

Random arrangement of Tintzl

Tintzl arranged to create areas of color

Tintzl combed into linear design

Tintzl coaxed into a shape

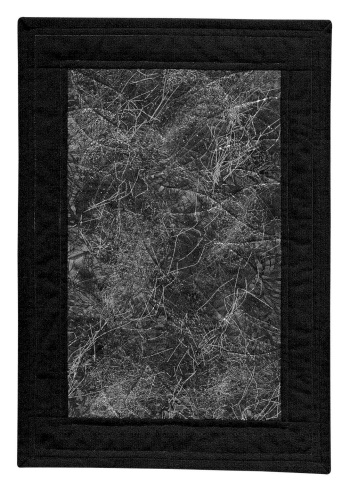

Cosmic Energy by Bonnie Lyn McCaffery, 1997, Hawley, Pennsylvania, 16" x 23". Tintzl is the only item on this quilt.

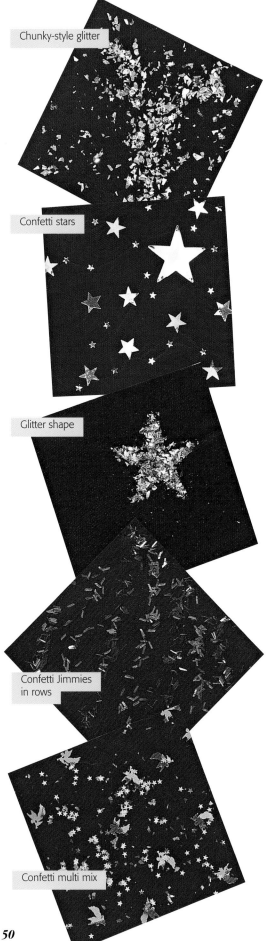

Chunky-style glitter

Confetti stars

Glitter shape

Confetti Jimmies
in rows

Confetti multi mix

Glitter

Glitter is another wonderful addition to fantasy fabrics. Keep in mind, how-ever, that the glitter must be large enough so it does not filter through the holes in the top layer, which is often tulle. Larger, chunkier glitter will not fall through the small mesh of finer tulle. Or, use a chiffon for the top layer when using fine glitter. The chiffon, however, will filter out some of the sparkle.

Caution: Do not let glitter particles fall into your machine. When you are finished stitching anything with glitter, clean the machine and remove any particles that may have fallen from between the layers. Be careful when pinning the layers together and use more pins than you think are necessary, especially around the edge of the piece. If you have any concerns about glitter falling into the machine, do not use glitter.

Sprinkle glitter randomly on the base fabric, or contain it in a specific shape. To make a glitter shape, use a cutout window template to limit where the glitter falls.

Pin the layers together, and keep the piece as flat as possible. Use a stiff stabilizer underneath the base fabric. To contain the glitter in a specific location, stitch around the edge of the piece first, then around the glittered areas. Once the glitter is secure, stitch remaining areas as desired.

Another thing to keep in mind when using glitter is that, once the quilted piece is hung on the wall (or worn in a garment), gravity will pull the glitter to the lowest horizontal line of stitching

If the stitching is too sparse, the glitter will fall into widely separated sections. More stitching will make smaller areas of allover glitter.

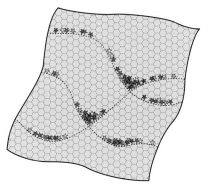

Metallic Confetti Shapes and Sequins

Metallic confetti shapes and sequins are available in a wide variety of color, size, and shape: stars, hearts, moons, masks, trees, and animals to name just a few. You can buy a variety of confetti mixes, such as holiday, party, island, or seasonal themes, or create your own mixes. Imagine the interesting effects you can create with these items trapped under a layer of tulle.

Confetti Jimmies are little bits of rectangular confetti that come in a full range of colors. They can be sprinkled randomly or arranged in colored rows. Like glitter, Jimmies require a lot of stitching to keep them in place.

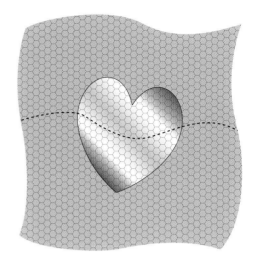

It is simple to incorporate metallic confetti and sequins into fantasy fabric. Position the shapes as desired. Be sure to separate the shapes because they tend to stick together; you don't want to stitch through more than one. Pin the top layer in place and stitch. Try to stitch through the larger shapes to hold them in position.

Like glitter, any unstitched pieces will eventually fall to the line of stitching below them. Add more stitching to keep confetti and sequins in the desired areas.

Caution: Pressing may dull the finish of the metallic shapes or melt the plastic ones. Test before pressing the finished piece. Either use a medium-temperature iron protected by a piece of copier paper, or do not press at all.

Christmas Tree (detail). Full quilt on page 76.

Holographic Paper and Stickers

Holographic paper or prism foil has a wonderful dimensional gleam. It comes in some beautiful colors as well as silver, which appears multicolored when turned in the light. There is usually a release liner attached to this "paper." It is called paper, but I'm sure it has plastic in it, so be careful with the iron.

Cut the shapes from the paper. For more precise shapes, trace the design on the release side of the holographic paper. Remember: you will need to draw the design in reverse. Cut out the design with scissors, an X-Acto knife, or a rotary cutter (depending on the intricacy of the shape).

Heart stickers

Triangles of different-colored holographic paper

Curved slivers of holographic paper

Accurate cut shape from holographic paper

TIP

Keep an extra rotary cutter and pair of scissors for cutting paper and other unusual things like holographic paper. Mark the handles with an indelible marker so you know these are for cutting paper.

I prefer to cut shapes without a pattern. Shapes can be geometric like squares, triangles, and circles, or more free-form like teardrops, curved slivers, and spirals. Once the shapes are cut, decide on their placement. Peel away the release liner and stick the pieces in place.

Add the top layer of tulle and stitch. Do not fold pieces containing holographic shapes. It is very difficult to remove fold lines from the holographic paper.

"How Sweet It Is" uses holographic-paper shapes within the fantasy fabrics.

Caution: The iron may do strange things to holographic paper, so be sure to test before pressing the finished piece. Press from the back and protect the holographic paper with a sheet of paper. Or, avoid pressing where the shapes are positioned.

Stickers are another wonderful option for fantasy fabrics. All sorts of designs are available. It is best to use these only in wall hangings or items that will not receive a lot of abuse or need cleaning. Once the stickers have been incorporated into the fantasy fabric, avoid folding the fabric. It is very difficult to remove fold lines from stickers.

How Sweet It Is by Bonnie Lyn McCaffery, 1998, Hawley, Pennsylvania, 54" x 43". Minced scraps, holographic paper, ribbons, scrunched fabric, and drizzled metallic thread are used in only four fantasy fabrics. These were then pieced and appliquéd. This quilt was in the works when I found out I was the recipient of the Jewel Pearce Patterson Scholarship that sent me to International Quilt Festival in Innsbruck, Austria. How Sweet It Is!

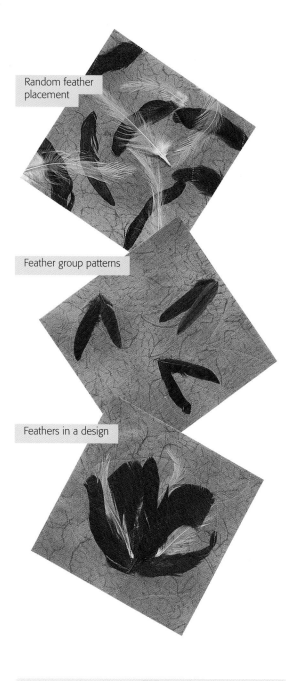

Random feather placement

Feather group patterns

Feathers in a design

Feathers

Feathers come in a great assortment of colors, sizes, and shapes. You can buy packages of them in craft stores and fishing departments. Some of them are sold individually, such as peacock feathers. I've also seen some very pretty feather dusters. Look for feathers during walks in the woods, or gather them from the bottom of the birdcage. Once you begin to search, you will see them everywhere.

Use feathers as they are or cut them into desired shapes. Arrange them randomly for an allover effect, or group them into a single design or an interesting repeat pattern. Stitch completely around a feather or a group of feathers to hold them in place. I used peacock feathers to create the design in "Wealth and Pride."

The eye of a peacock feather has a tendency to separate. To hold it together, lightly coat the back of the feather with white glue. Let the glue dry completely before adding the feather to the design.

The sewing-machine needle also has a tendency to separate feather parts. If this separation is going to bother you, do not stitch over the feather.

TIP

If you are using prepackaged feathers, remove them from the bag one at a time, selecting the best in the bag. Do not empty the bag onto the background fabric because excess color chunks and stray feathers may spoil the design. It is difficult to remove these once they have come in contact with the base fabric.

Wealth and Pride (detail). Full quilt on page 61.

Charms, Beads, and Other Bulkies

Charms, beads, shells, polished stones, and ribbon roses add a delightful dimension to any fantasy fabric. They are a good choice for fabrics that will be used as wall hangings or for larger pieces. Since these items cannot be cut or stitched through, it is best not to use them in a large piece of fabric that will be randomly cut up and pieced or appliquéd.

You can use these items in appliquéd or pieced projects, but you must be careful about their placement. Mark the stitching line before creating the fantasy fabric. Keep the items well within the line, and stitch around them to hold them in place. Position items at least ¼" away from any seam lines. The sewing-machine foot needs a flat space to stitch and will not ride up over a charm, bead, or shell. You can use the foot as a guide along the edge of the items being stitched. To stitch even closer to the items being captured, shift the needle position.

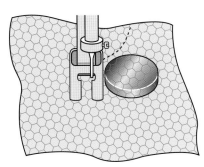

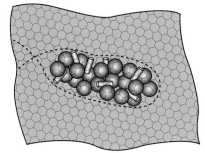

Since these items are bulky, be careful when stitching the layers together. The machine will not react well if you run over these things. Stitch completely around the items to hold them in place.

Charms

Charms can add interest to your fantasy fabric, but they will add weight to your finished project, so limit their use.

Many brass charms become dull with time. Before adding them to the fantasy fabric, polish them with a brass polish. Rub and buff them to a shine, then spray with a clear acrylic sealer to maintain the shine. Let the sealer dry completely before stitching the charm in place.

Arrange charms on the base fabric as desired and top with the usual layer of tulle. Surround them with lots of pins so they will stay in position. If the charms move, you can easily push them back into place as you are stitching.

Carefully stitch around the charms. Avoid hitting them with the needle because it will definitely bend or break the needle. If possible, hold a finger on the charm to keep it from slipping out of place, but keep your fingers out of the way of the needle. Or, use an orange stick or the eraser end of a pencil to hold the charm while stitching. Stitch completely around the charm to ensure it stays in position.

Pearls, ribbon roses, ribbons, and Tintzl under yellow tulle

Charms and Tintzl under green tulle

Beads, pearls, and Tintzl under white tulle

Seashells, beads, and Tintzl under blue tulle

Beads

Many of the smaller varieties of beads can be captured under a layer of tulle. Seed beads, bugle beads, pearls, and gold beads are all good choices. There are two things to keep in mind when selecting beads to use in fantasy fabric. They must not be so small that they will migrate through the holes in the tulle, and they must not be so large that the tulle will not conform around them. Six millimeters is probably the largest diameter that you can use without causing distortion to the tulle and adding excess weight to the piece.

One way to add beads is to sprinkle them on the base fabric. Add a layer of tulle and pin as much as needed to hold the beads in place. They will move, so it's important to surround areas of beads or individual larger beads with a line of stitching.

Do not run over the beads with the sewing-machine foot or the needle. If the beads move, you can gently push them back into place as long as the stitching allows. Remember that beads, like glitter, are going to fall to the lowest horizontal line of stitching when the piece is held vertically. With this in mind, be sure to add enough stitching so beads will fall as you desire.

Another way to add beads is to stitch a channel to contain them. Leave an opening on one side at the edge of the fabric. Pour the beads into the channel and move them with your finger into place. Stitch the end of the channel closed so the beads do not leak out the side.

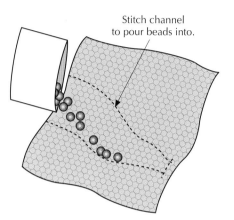

Stitch channel to pour beads into.

Shells and Polished Stones

Why not capture a little nature into your fantasy fabric? You can buy packages of tiny shells and pebbles in craft stores or collect them along the shore. Thoroughly wash and completely dry shells and pebbles. Make sure the edges are smooth. Rough edges or sharp points will cut into the top layer of fabric.

Treat shells like charms when incorporating them into a piece of fantasy fabric. Just remember, shells are fragile. Avoid pressing down on them or they will break. Pebbles can be treated the same way as beads.

Pre-Made Ribbon Roses

Ribbon roses come in a wide assortment of colors. They are the quickest and easiest of the bulky items to use in fantasy fabric. Since they are made of ribbon, you won't break a needle if you accidentally stitch into one.

Arrange the roses on the base fabric as desired. Use a dab of temporary basting glue if you want to be certain that the roses don't move. Place the layer of tulle on top and pin well around the roses to hold them in place. Stitch close to the roses, using the sewing-machine foot as a guide. Be sure all roses are completely surrounded by stitching.

Silk Flowers

One of the most popular items to incorporate into fantasy fabric is silk flowers. They are available in a variety of colors, shapes, and sizes. Pansies, dogwood, lilacs, daisies, and cosmos are just a few of the possibilities that work well in fantasy fabrics.

When selecting silk flowers, do not choose flowers with metal wire in the petals. Keep in mind how the flower will look once it is pressed between two layers of fabric. Press petals open and flat, or fold them on top of each other as they come on the stem. While roses are truly beautiful, they are not the best choice for fantasy fabric. When roses are pressed open, they lose their shape and no longer look like roses. And if they are layered as they come on the stem, they will be too bulky.

To use silk flowers, first separate them from the plastic stem. Sometimes there will be little plastic separators between layers of petals. Be sure to remove these as well. In general, remove plastic parts from the flower to avoid excessive bulk and to allow the petals to lie flat. Restack flower petals or arrange them separately on the base.

Be sure to include leaves in a floral design to give it a more natural appearance. Peel leaves from the plastic stem to which they are attached. You can use narrow ribbon to create stems if you want to connect the leaves. Long, thin leaves are a great way to connect one area to another without using any stems. You can also use leaves by themselves to create some interesting leafy prints.

Group tiny flowers, like lilacs, to give a natural appearance. Seed beads make a perfect center for these flowers.

Observe how the silk flowers appear on the stems before taking them apart so they will look natural when you put them back together. Arrange flowers by size, from larger at the base of the stem to small buds at the end. Overlapping petals here and there will add dimension to the design.

Once the design is in place, add the top layer. Pin as often as needed to hold the flowers in place. Do not pin into the flowers. Pins may leave undesirable holes in silk flowers.

Allover pattern of flowers

Natural grouping of flowers

Ivy leaves

Line of flowers from small to large

Grouping of tiny flowers

Fantasy Floral Kaleidoscope by Bonnie Lyn McCaffery, 1998, Hawley, Pennsylvania, 25" x 30". Silk flowers and leaves were added to an existing background.

Stitch the layers together, but do not stitch on the edge of the silk flowers, which may cause them to fray. Instead, stitch around the outside of the flower, or take a few stitches into the center of the flower. If you know a certain flower is going to fray, use Fray Check to stop the fraying. Let it dry completely before stitching the layers together.

Add beads and buttons to the center of flowers for a perfect finish. Use tiny seed beads, pearls, or metallic beads. Sew one bead or button to a flower, or sew several in a group.

A few silk flowers and ivy leaves add an interesting touch to "Fantasy Floral Kaleidoscope." The background for this piece was actually a UFO (unfinished object) that had been in my cabinet for ages. I put it together in a day. Since this is a wall hanging, I even left the plastic stems on the ivy.

A floral scene or bouquet can be created in fantasy fabric in a fraction of the time it would take to do an appliqué piece and makes a beautiful quilt. "Fantasy Bouquet" incorporates a variety of different flowers. The vase was cut from a piece of cotton fabric, and a few pieces of a gold knit fabric were added for accents.

Fantasy Bouquet (detail). Single beads and clustered beads fill the center of these flowers. Long slender leaves act as a connection between flowers. Full quilt on page 60.

Doll Hair

I thought I covered everything possible to be captured under a layer of tulle. Then Barbara Anderson, who had taken my class, gave me a package of curly doll hair. Well, why not?

Arrange the doll hair as you would any other object, but play with it to give it a natural appearance. Add the top layer of tulle, pin, then stitch. The hair tends to be bulky, making it difficult to stitch through. Stitch around it and occasionally into the hair edges to hold it in place.

Add some flowers or a fancy rhinestone barrette (just a line of rhinestones) after stitching the layers together. Cover the edge of the hair with a hat if desired.

Curly doll hair was used in "Contemplation II: Midnight Rendezvous."

Contemplation II: Midnight Rendezvous by Bonnie Lyn McCaffery, 1998, Hawley, Pennsylvania, 33" x 41". Curly hair, carefully cut shapes, and ribbon and silk flowers make up the little girl sitting on a vinyl fabric bench. Her dress is a piece of fantasy fabric. Creative Crystals rhinestones are the stars in the sky. The constellations of Libra (my husband) and Scorpio (me) appear in the sky. Libra represents balance and Scorpio, determination. The little girl and the cat contemplate from where they came. Aren't we all just star stuff?

Wealth and Pride (above) by Bonnie Lyn McCaffery, 1997, Hawley, Pennsylvania, 22" x 24½". Peacock feathers are captured on a luxurious gold base fabric. Creative Crystals rhinestones add sparkle. It is bordered with a metallic decorated velvet. The luxurious fabric and peacock feathers symbolize things we often aspire to, but the narrow burlap border is a reminder of our more humble beginnings

Fantasy Bouquet (left) by Bonnie Lyn McCaffery, 1998, Hawley, Pennsylvania, 41" x 50". Numerous silk flowers are formed into a bouquet. Tintzl was sprinkled onto the background. Beads finish the flowers nicely. The final border is done with suede cloth and Kreiniks metallic ribbon.

Adding Items to the Top Layer

Some of the same items that can be captured between layers can also be added to the top layer of fantasy fabrics. But there are many other treasures you can add, such as dangling beads and tassels, that you wouldn't think of stitching between the layers. Don't consider a piece of fantasy fabric finished just because it's been stitched and quilted. The sky's the limit when it comes to adding even more wonderful items to the top of fantasy fabrics.

Buttons, Beads, Rhinestones, and Metallic Studs

Buttons, beads, rhinestones, and studs are really just dots in design terms. They can be scattered in random fashion to add overall texture. Or, they can be carefully placed to accent specific shapes. Try arranging them in circles or meandering lines to add another dimensional design to a piece. The design ideas for each of these are interchangeable. Keep in mind that when a button is mentioned for a flower center, you can easily substitute beads, rhinestones, or studs.

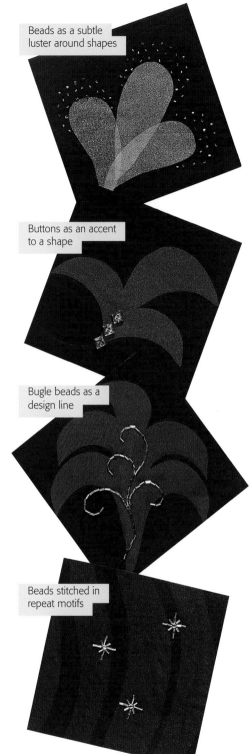

Beads as a subtle luster around shapes

Buttons as an accent to a shape

Bugle beads as a design line

Beads stitched in repeat motifs

Buttons

Beautiful buttons, standard shirt buttons, funny buttons, metal buttons, sparkly buttons—these are just a few of the available choices. Sew them to the center of flowers or at the base of a teardrop design.

Buttons can be added before basting or after quilting. The decision is based on whether they will be in the way during quilting. It is easier to stitch on buttons and hide the knots before assembling the quilt layers. But consider whether they will be in the way of the quilt hoop or the sewing-machine foot while trying to quilt. If they are added after the quilting, hide the knots under the buttons, and stitch only through the top quilt layer without going into the backing.

Leave knot on surface if button will cover it.

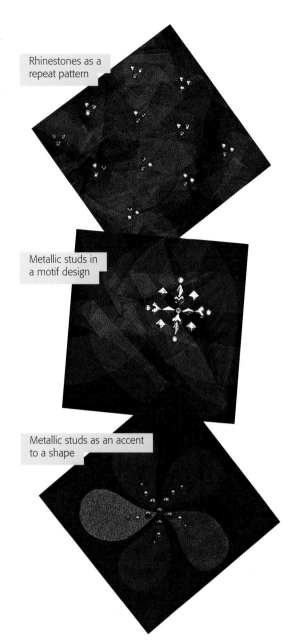

Rhinestones as a repeat pattern

Metallic studs in a motif design

Metallic studs as an accent to a shape

Beads

Beads, like buttons, come in a great variety. Seed beads, bugle beads, pearls, crystals, metallic beads, wooden beads, and alphabet beads are just a few. Stitch beads randomly onto the background to add a subtle luster, or arrange them to create a design, such as curved lines or stars. The beads in "Bubblin' Up II" (page 20) accent the shapes and add lustrous highlights.

Again, you must decide whether to add beads before or after quilting. The beads may get in the way of the hoop and sewing-machine foot. When sewing the beads, bury the knot under the top layer of the quilt, and do not stitch through to the back of the quilt. Use a sturdy thread, such as quilting thread, to attach the beads. Just be sure the thread will go through the hole in the bead. I usually match the thread color to the base fabric or use transparent nylon thread. Go through the bead two or three times to ensure that the bead will stay in place. Take a tiny backstitch before knotting and burying the end of the thread.

You can also glue beads to the surface with a dot of glue. Be sure to use a glue that is specifically made for attaching beads to fabric. Gem Tac is a favorite of those who add beads to bridal accessories.

Kathleen Porycki had lots of fun adding buttons, beads, and rhinestones to her "Fantasy Fabric, Thread, Buttons, and Beads" wall hanging. She also glued large rhinestones to the top of standard white buttons.

Rhinestones and Metallic Studs

Creative Crystals has beautiful pre-glued crystal rhinestones, pearls, and metallic shapes. You must use a Bejeweler to melt the glue on the back of the crystal, pearl, or metallic shape before positioning it in place. Install the appro-

priate-size tip on the Bejeweler and preheat it. Pick up a stone on the end of the tip. Let the glue melt until it is bubbly, then press it into place. Using the Bejeweler is very easy to do and much better than using regular glue, which tends to ooze up around the edge of the stone.

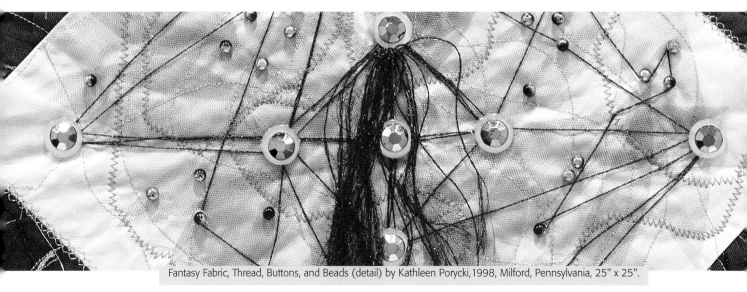

Fantasy Fabric, Thread, Buttons, and Beads (detail) by Kathleen Porycki, 1998, Milford, Pennsylvania, 25" x 25".

Rhinestones, pearls, and metallic shapes can be used in the same manner as beads or buttons. Arrange them randomly or in design lines, individually or in clusters. You can also create your own design or accent other shapes in the piece.

Dangles

All kinds of wonderful things can be dangled from fantasy fabrics (or any other quilts for that matter). Just take a walk down the aisles of your favorite craft store and you will find lots of items. I'll give you just a few ideas to think about and try.

If the fabric will be used for piecing, attach the dangles after piecing. You can add the dangles before or after quilting, depending on how many items there are and whether they will get in the way of the quilt hoop or sewing-machine foot. If you add them after the quilting, remember to bury the knot between the layers.

Charms and Dangling Beads

The first sample includes several beads hanging from ⅛"-wide metallic ribbon. The dangling beads are easy to assemble. Use a large-eyed needle to accommodate the ribbon. Tie a knot in one of the ribbon ends before bringing the needle through to the top. Thread a large bead on the ribbon, followed by a smaller bead; then pass the needle back through the large bead. The smaller bead acts as a stopper.

Manipulate the beads on the ribbon to achieve the desired length, and thread the ribbon to the back of the fabric. Double-check the length of the dangle before tying a knot in the back. Add additional hanging beads in the same fashion, but vary the lengths of ribbon.

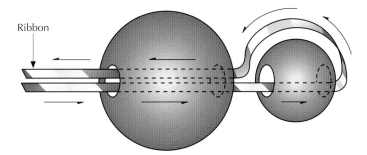

Ribbon

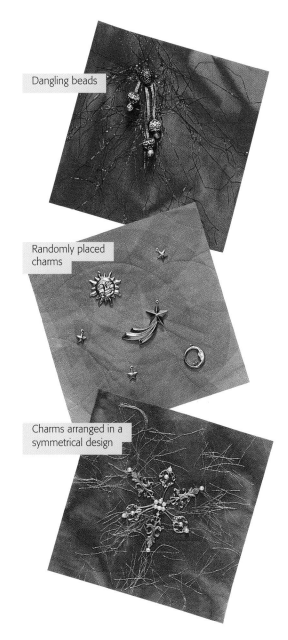

Dangling beads

Randomly placed charms

Charms arranged in a symmetrical design

In a previous section, you learned how to capture charms under a layer of tulle. But they can also be stitched to the top of the fabric to add a bit of whimsy and personality to a quilt. Don't forget to polish brass charms as described on page 55. For an interesting touch, try adding a bead when attaching the charm. You will cover the hole in the charm and add another element to the project.

Threads and Tassels

Unusual textures can be added to fantasy fabrics with dangling threads. Select a group of threads and cut a 15" piece from each one. Thread them all through a needle with an eye large enough to accommodate all threads. Without knotting the threads, take a stitch into the fabric from the top, leaving about a 3" tail. Take a second stitch over the first (like a backstitch) and tie the ends in a knot. Trim the ends to the desired length and let them dangle. Additional stitched knots can be done without having to rethread the needle.

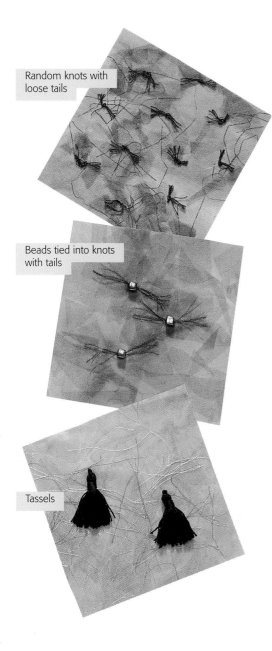

Random knots with loose tails

Beads tied into knots with tails

Tassels

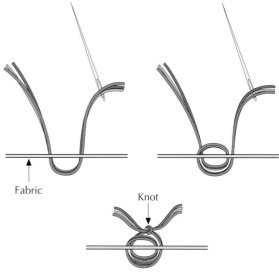

Fabric

Knot

For more interest, add a bead with a hole large enough to accommodate the threads before knotting and cutting the ends. Take a stitch from the top of the fabric. Add a bead. Take a second stitch. Go through the bead again. Tie the thread ends in a knot. Work the knot into the hole of the bead. Add a dab of glue to keep the knot inside the bead. Cut the thread tails to the desired length.

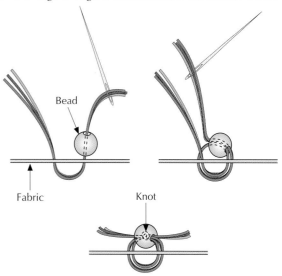

Bead

Fabric

Knot

Tassels add another textural element to a quilt. Choose from a great selection of pre-made tassels, or make your own. There are several beautiful books on how to make tassels. For inspiration, look at the tassel made of Candlelight metallic yarn in the center of Kathleen Porycki's "Fantasy Fabric, Thread, Buttons, and Beads" wall hanging on page 64.

66

Using Fantasy Fabrics

Now that you have created this unique fabric, what can you do with it? There are so many wonderful ways to use your fantasy fabrics. Only a few are discussed here. There are, however, a few limitations to using fantasy fabrics. Since you probably used some nonstandard objects and fabrics, the finished fantasy fabric may be stiff or bulky.

Careful thought is needed to use this newly created fabric for clothing, piecing, appliqué, and bindings (as discussed in each section). Bulky items cannot be cut into or stitched and are not good for random piecing and randomly cut appliqué pieces. Items used in clothing must be carefully considered for durability and washability. Each of these limitations will be covered in the section pertaining to its use.

Art

If you want to treat your fantasy fabric as a piece of art, simply attach borders to frame the piece, add some embellishments, and quilt it. That's what I did with "Out of the Darkness." Framing a piece is an excellent way to finish a fantasy fabric, whether it's a realistic scene or an abstract design.

Out of the Darkness by Bonnie Lyn McCaffery, 1998, Hawley, Pennsylvania, 51" x 40". Various cut sheers and metallic gold tricot-lamé moon slivers radiate upward on a hand-painted fabric background accented with Tintzl and metallic threads.

Backgrounds

Fantasy fabric may be the perfect background for a scene or an abstract design. You can appliqué directly onto the surface. You can also use a piece of fantasy fabric as the base fabric for another piece of fantasy fabric. A scrunched fantasy fabric became the perfect midnight sky in "Contemplation I."

Contemplation I by Bonnie Lyn McCaffery, 1998, Hawley, Pennsylvania, 25" x 30". A scrunched sheer fantasy fabric acts as a background to the fairy. Creative Crystals rhinestones are added as stars in the night sky. Suede cloth and felt were cut into flowers and leaves. The fairy (as a winged creature) contemplates where she came from, perhaps once being a caterpillar herself. This quilt evolved after I received the Jewel Pearce Patterson Scholarship to attend The International Quilt Festival in Austria. The fairy could easily represent me as I imagine the quilting journey I am on—where I've been and where I'm going.

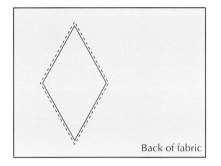

Back of fabric

Pieced Designs

More fun begins when you think of your fantasy fabric as you would any other beautiful fabric. Before cutting the fantasy fabric into pieces, ask yourself a few questions. How small are the captured elements? Are any of the captured elements uncuttable or unstitchable? Are the captured elements going to stay in place? How small do I want to cut the pieces? Are the stitching lines close enough to keep the layers together? If the cut pieces are fairly large (3" and up), and the layers were stitched at about 1" intervals, there should be no problem. However, you may need to do more stitching before you cut the pieces. If captured elements look too loose or as though they might fall out, more stitching may be required. Once the pieces are cut, handle them with care until all open edges have been stitched closed.

Another option is to use a template to trace the finished-size piece (without seam allowances) on the wrong side of the fantasy fabric, and add a straight line of stitching just beyond the drawn line. This will contain the captured items within the edges as it is cut and pieced into a design.

Hoffman Fantasy Stars by Bonnie Lyn McCaffery, 1998, Hawley, Pennsylvania, 49" x 42". All the warm-colored stars are made from fantasy fabrics. Nubby yarn, Tintzl, metallic thread, metallic confetti, rayon floss, and strip piecing were used to create the fabric.

Add ¼"-wide seam allowances beyond the drawn line and cut out the piece. Then stitch as usual.

"Hoffman Fantasy Stars" was created by strip piecing 4" strips of fantasy fabrics alternately with cool-colored fabrics. Stitching the strips together helped to control the threads and keep the confetti from falling out. The triangles were then cut and pieced together.

"How Sweet It Is" (page 53) incorporates four pieces of fantasy fabric. Most of the quilt was pieced, but one curve was appliquéd.

Appliqué Designs

These sparkling fantasy fabrics can also be used for appliqué. They will need to be handled with a little more care than ordinary fabrics.

Keep in mind the distance between the stitching lines holding the layers together, as well as the size of the intended appliqué piece. Add more stitching to keep the captured items in place and the layers together if necessary. Use a template to trace the shape onto the wrong side of the fantasy fabric. Stitch just beyond the drawn line as described in the "Pieced Designs" section above. Once the edges are stitched, cut out the piece, adding a ¼" to ⅜" seam allowance all around.

Turn under the edges of the piece and pin or thread-baste. Finger pressing and needle turning are not good methods to use when appliquéing fantasy-fabric pieces. There may be several layers of fabric to turn under, so you will need to thread-baste or pin to keep the layers together.

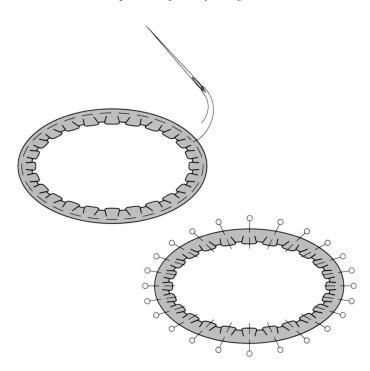

Caution: Remember when pressing these fabrics to be careful about the temperature of the iron, and to protect the surface of the iron. I keep inexpensive copier paper handy to cover any parts I may have doubts about.

TIP

Here's a great way to make perfect circles. Tape a thumbtack, point side up, to the left of the sewing-machine needle, on the machine base. The distance from the tack to the needle will be the radius of the circle. Place the fabric on top of the tack so that the point comes through the fabric. Place an eraser on the tack to protect yourself. As you stitch, pivot the fabric on the tack. Voilà—a perfect circle.

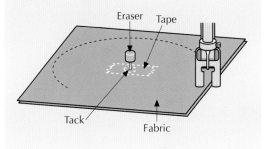

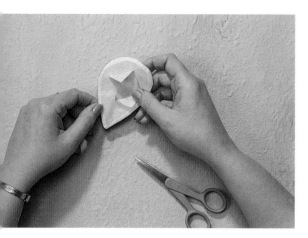

Another technique for larger, uncomplicated appliqué shapes eliminates the need to stitch around the edge. This technique should only be used on straight edges or gently curved shapes with no sharp points. Trace the design onto the wrong side of the fantasy fabric. Place another piece of similarly colored cotton fabric or lightweight interfacing on top of the fantasy fabric with right sides together. Stitch on the drawn line without leaving an opening. Trim the edges to just under ¼". Trim the excess fabric from any points, and clip any curves as necessary to make the piece lie flat once it has been turned right side out. Carefully cut an X in the regular fabric or interfacing. Do not cut the fantasy fabric.

Turn the piece right side out. Use a Purple Thang (a plastic tool with a rounded point used to push turned corners out and smooth seams) or other point-turning tool to smooth the stitched edge and push points out. Press with a medium-temperature setting on the wrong side of the fantasy fabric. Remember to protect the ironing surface if the piece contains unusual items. The piece is now ready to appliqué in place by hand or machine.

I used this appliqué technique to add the circles in "Genesis: A New Beginning."

Fantasy Fabric Sampler

It is so much fun making fantasy fabric that you might want to make several pieces to try different techniques. Why not play with squares of fabric? Cut several 8" squares of various colors of tulle and base fabrics. Experiment with different combinations of base fabrics, captured items, and top layers. Once the fantasy fabrics are made, cut the squares to size and sew them together into a fantasy sampler.

Laurie used her sample blocks in a piece she calls "Dancing on the Delaware."

Dancing on the Delaware (above) by Laurie D. Calvitti, 1998, Hawley, Pennsylvania, 35½" x 17½". "These three first pieces from Bonnie's class kept running together like the river—no matter how often I tried to separate them. They reminded me of the beauty and abundant life you see on a rafting trip, between the granite walls and sandy beaches."

Fantasy Class Sampler (right) by Bonnie Lyn McCaffery, 1998, Hawley, Pennsylvania, 11½" x 33". Grouped Candlelight Yarn snips, feathers, Tintzl, metallic confetti, and cut sheers create this sampling of fantasy fabrics.

Genesis: A New Beginning (left) by Bonnie Lyn McCaffery, 1998, Hawley, Pennsylvania, 39" x 29". The entire piece is made from fantasy fabrics with a base of only black or white. The "trumpet" shapes radiating from the corner were created using tulle as a background and snipped metallic floss between the layers. Even the binding and border are made from fantasy fabrics. The gradated background uses several colors of tulle. Tintzl and metallic thread were also incorporated into the fabrics.

Borders

Many times we come to the point of adding borders to a quilt and wish we had just the right fabric. Why not create just the right-color fabric to go with the central portion of the quilt? If you have a fabric that is close, but you wish it were a little darker, a little lighter, or a little greener, fantasy fabric can be the solution. Create your fantasy fabric, then cut and sew as you would any other border.

Judy Levine created a perfect fantasy-fabric border for "Wind Dance." Notice how the colors gradate from light in one corner to a little darker in the opposite corner. She did this by adding more layers and using darker colors toward the upper right corner.

Wind Dance by Judy Zoelzer Levine, 1996, Bayside, Wisconsin, 33½" x 40". Silk organzas on a cotton background. Overlapping colors create additional colors and depth. The border is made from thinner strips of the same organzas and is stitched in ⅛" channels.

Bindings

You can also use fantasy-fabric techniques to create the perfect binding to match your quilt top. Not all fantasy fabrics can be used as bindings, however. Those that have stiffer items like confetti shapes, sequins, holographic paper, or silk flowers may not be appropriate since they are bulky and will not fold well. Fantasy fabrics with sheers, threads, and Tintzl work much better.

Double-check to see if there is sufficient stitching to hold the layers together while cutting strips. To be safe, mark cutting lines for the strips before cutting them, then stitch ¼" from both sides of the marked lines. You can then cut the strips apart without the captured items falling out. Use your favorite method to attach the binding.

"Genesis: A New Beginning" (page 72) and "Sherbet Surprise" (page 21) both have bindings created from fantasy fabric.

Clothing

Why not use some of this wonderful fabric in clothing? Just be sure to consider the items that have been used in making the fantasy fabric. Cleaning the garment may be a problem. Metallic fabrics don't respond well to dry cleaning; other fabrics may not wash well. Try to use fabrics and items that will tolerate the same cleaning method. Many can be gently hand washed, but test before spending a lot of time making a spectacular garment, only to find that once it's soiled, it can't be worn again.

You can make a whole garment out of fantasy fabric, or combine portions of fantasy fabric with other fabrics to add great focus areas. Vests are a perfect way to try some of the fantasy fabric in clothing and to show off some of your newly created fabrics.

Barbara Anderson created and used some gorgeous fantasy fabric for a mock collar on a vest.

Covering buttons with fantasy fabric might be the perfect touch for a simple piece of clothing. Make sure the buttonhole is large enough to accommodate the button with its extra fabric. It should also be loose enough so it doesn't cause excess friction on the fabric. Since buttons are rather small, use fantasy fabrics that have smaller elements in them, such as Tintzl and snipped or drizzled threads. What a perfect way to finish off a garment!

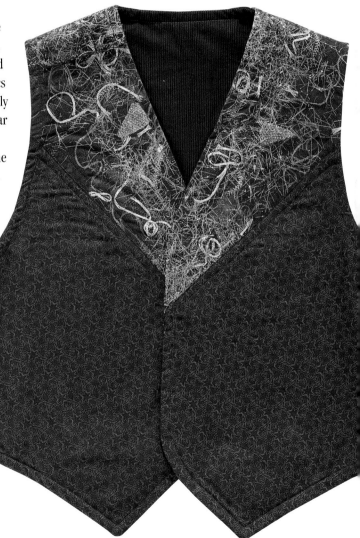

Vest by Barbara Anderson, 1998, Dingmans Ferry, Pennsylvania. Ribbons, Tintzl, metallic confetti shapes, and snips of large-hole tulle create a sparkling piece of fabric on this vest.

Children's Projects

Christmas Tree by Shelby M. Gallagher (age 7) with the help of Marie B. DiGerlando (grandmother), 1998, Westbrookville, New York. Shelby was given a tree shape at Christmas and was told to trim it any way she wanted. After seeing what Marie had done in the Fantasy Fabric class, Shelby wanted to trim her tree in that style. She trimmed the tree and Marie did the quilting. Needless to say, her tree outshined everyone else's, which made her very happy because she always likes to feel like a star.

Making fantasy fabric is a fantastic project to do with children. Cut out a green Christmas-tree shape for the base fabric and let the kids add the toppings. They love glitzy stuff like glitter and will have a great time decorating the tree. Add the top layer and have an adult do the stitching. It's a perfect way to share a good time and make something the child will be proud of.

Accessories

Fantasy fabric is the perfect fabric for some of those glitzy occasions. The lovely prom purse shown below was made by my daughter, Heather McCaffery, to go with her prom dress of soft green and black velvet. She used a solid black fabric for the base. She then added Tintzl, some holographic paper, and a few stars, and topped it all with a light green tulle. The stitching was done with holographic sliver thread, adding just a little more sparkle. To make a strap, she added a string of rhinestones. She created fabric that matched her prom dress while making a one-of-a-kind purse to enhance her high-school memory.

Prom Purse (above) by Heather Lyn McCaffery, 1998, Hawley, Pennsylvania, 10" x 6⅜". Holographic paper, holographic Tintzl, and holographic metallic stars twinkle in this fantasy fabric purse.

Whenever I think of jewelry, I think of sparkle. I made this abstract necklace by creating a small piece of fantasy fabric with that all-time favorite sparkly material: Tintzl. I then backed the fabric and turned it right side out. A bead at the top, a cord, and a few rhinestones completed this fun necklace.

Necklace (right) by Bonnie Lyn McCaffery, 1998, Hawley, Pennsylvania. Tintzl and Creative Crystals rhinestones make this fantasy necklace.

Why not a pin? Or a necklace with numerous pieces of fantasy fabric hanging from it? Or maybe some bookmarks? Barbara Anderson created a piece of fun fabric that she used to cover a photo album. The flowered fabric was actually a printed sheer. She finished the piece by stitching green lace around the design.

Kathy Oehlmann created a unique checkbook cover with a piece of fantasy fabric she created in class.

Checkbook Cover (above) by Kathy Oehlmann, 1998, Dingmans Ferry, Pennsylvania. Cut metallic fabric, ribbon, stars, Tintzl, and fairy stickers are used in the fabric.

Fantasy Photo Album (right) by Barbara Anderson, 1998, Dingmans Ferry, Pennsylvania, 7¾" x 12½". A floral printed sheer fabric was cut and captured along with Tintzl and green lace.

You could use fantasy fabrics for place mats with matching napkin rings, pillows, or Christmas stockings. How about a tote bag or an eyeglasses case? You could jazz up last year's prom dress or maybe that blazer with the food stain. Oh, the endless possibilities! Play with the process. I'm sure you'll think of things to capture under a layer of tulle that I haven't begun to imagine. It's quick, it's fun, and it's instantly rewarding. You will be captivated and mesmerized into creativity. Have fun with it, and by all means, let me know of anything I have missed.

Resources

Creative Crystals Co.

PO Box 8
Unionville, CT 06085
(800) 578-0716
*Bejeweler, Creative Crystals rhinestones
and metal trims*

eQuilter

Luana Rubin
4581 Maple Court
Boulder, CO 80301
(303) 516-1615
www.eQuilter.com
e-mail:luana@eQuilter.com
*Online store for Tintzl, quilting fabrics,
and accessories. Specializing in Asian-
Pacific and contemporary fabrics, supplying
the quilt and fabric-artist markets.*

Kreinik Manufacturing

3106 Timanus Lane, Suite 101
Baltimore, MD 21244
(800) 537-2166
Metallic cord, ribbons, and braids

Loose Ends

(503) 390-7457
www.4loosends.com
Pulp Netting, Abaca Fibre, and Banana Wrap

Speed Stitch (Sulky)

3113-D Broadpoint Drive
Harbor Heights, FL 33983
(800) 874-4115
Sulky products

Web of Thread

1410 Broadway
Paducah, KY 42001
(800) 955-8185
Specialty threads, ribbons

YLI Corporation

161 West Main Street
Rock Hill, SC 29730
(803) 985-3100
Candlelight yarn, threads, silk ribbons

Z-Barten Productions

8611 Hayden Place
Culver City, CA 90232
(310) 202-7070
*Glitter, confetti, Tintzl, Jimmie Jems,
feathers*

Bibliography

Eddy, Ellen Anne. *Thread Magic: The Enchanted World of Ellen Anne Eddy.* Bothell, Wash.:
    That Patchwork Place, Inc., 1997.
Fanning, Robbie and Tony Fanning. *The Complete Book of Machine Quilting.* Radnor, Pa.:
    Chilton Book Company, 1994.
Hatch, Sandra L., and Ann Boyce. *Putting on the Glitz.* Radnor, Pa.: Chilton Book Company,
    1991.
Hill, Wendy. *On the Surface.* Lafayette, Calif.: C&T Publishing, Inc., 1997.
Lehman, Libby. *Threadplay.* Bothell, Wash.: That Patchwork Place, Inc., 1997.
Murrah, Judy. *Jazz It Up: 101 Stitching & Embellishing Techniques.* Bothell, Wash.: Martingale
    & Company, 1998.
Noble, Maurine, and Elizabeth Hendricks. *Machine Quilting with Decorative Threads.* Bothell,
    Wash.: Martingale & Company, 1998.

About the Author

Quilting is Bonnie's life. She has been an active member of the Milford Valley Quilters Guild since it started ten years ago. Bonnie loves to design, lecture, and travel. She teaches at Quilters Attic in Pinebush, New York. She also lectures to quilt guilds throughout the country. Her specialties are fantasy fabric, kaleidoscope quilts, freeform appliqué quilts, and dimensional quilts. By no means traditional, these quilts are more like art pieces. She is always trying to stretch quilting to its limits.

In 1998, she was awarded the Jewel Pearce Patterson Scholarship to attend the European Quilt Market and the International Quilt Festival in Innsbruck, Austria. Only one U.S. quilter is selected each year to receive this prestigious award.

Her work has appeared in *American Quilters Society Magazine*, *Quilting International*, *Quilter's Newsletter Magazine*, and *Craftworks*. For four years, she designed craft projects for *Craftworks*. Working with craft projects kept her apprised of the wonderful products on the market—many of which she has incorporated into fantasy fabric.

Bonnie is the wife of Michael McCaffery and mother of three teenage daughters: Heather, Carly, and Abby. She loves music (especially New Age), cats, art, her computer, learning new things, New Age philosophy, and skiing.